GWR
B-1775

ROAD VEHICLES
of the
GREAT WESTERN RAILWAY

PHILIP J. KELLEY

Oxford Publishing Co · Oxford

SBN. 902888 12 9

Halftones and Plates
By Oxford Lithoplates Ltd.
Printed in the City of Oxford

Acknowledgements

My sincere thanks go to the following British Rail staff for their unfailing help in the preparation of this book: — Neil Sprinks, Public Relations Office, Paddington; C. Chilvers and C. Froud, Photographic Section, Swindon Works; W.R. MacDonald, Chief Civil Engineer's Office, Paddington; Harry Whatson, British Transport Historical Records; R.A.P. Cogger, Museum of British Transport, Clapham. Thanks also to A.T. Brackenborough, W.H. Castle, Vic Green, B. Harding, Frank Dumbleton and Keith Steele (who has spurred me on throughout). The following organisations have been of great assistance: — Scammell Lorries Ltd., A.E.C. Ltd., Radio Times Hulton Picture Library and particularly Mr. G.W. Dascombe of Transport Equipment (Thornycroft) Ltd. who has helped considerably with information and drawings concerning their vehicles. I owe more than I can say to Peter Thatcher for his hard work in producing the drawings for this album. John M. Cummings has been of great assistance, particularly regarding the omnibus section. Finally I must thank my father, C.J. Kelley, for his efforts in undertaking certain research on my behalf.

Philip J. Kelley 1972

Published by
Oxford Publishing Co.
5 Lewis Close,
Risinghurst, Headington,
Oxford.

Introduction

Many books have been written about the Great Western Railway but one aspect that hasn't been covered fully, is the vast collection of road vehicles, of many types, which comprised the Company's fleet. This album, it is hoped, will go some way towards filling this gap. It is not intended to be a concise history but more a pictorial record with the photographs, (many of which have not been published before) telling their own story. The drawings have been specially prepared and in certain cases some detail is subject to conjecture, due to lack of information available. They should be of assistance to modellers who wish to have an authentic scale model in their station yard.

The livery of G.W.R. road vehicles followed very closely that of the rail passenger carriages, being either chocolate brown & cream, chocolate brown or crimson lake according to the period. Some of the early omnibuses had just plain varnished wood bodies and a few were thought to have appeared in green. The lettering consisted of the full "Great Western Railway" or just the initials "G.W.R." either in gold leaf or cream with or without shading. The coat of arms was rarely used. The canvas tilt or hood, where fitted, was usually black with white unshaded lettering and, in some cases, space was provided for a company poster. There were many variations and exceptions to the above and where this is considered of interest they are noted under the photograph concerned.

The book has been compiled under four main headings: *(1) Horse drawn vehicles (2) Mechanically propelled cartage vehicles (3) Motor omnibuses 'Road motors' (4) Miscellaneous vehicles. There is an introduction to each section.*

Horses were used, of course, from the very beginning and later worked side by side with their mechanical brothers, right up to Nationalisation. The G.W.R. was undoubtedly one of the pioneers in using mechanically propelled road vehicles, first for cartage in 1902 and for passengers in 1903. Many experimental units were tried using different methods of propulsion. The mechanical horse and trailer were the final stage in the development before the Great Western Railway went out of existence in 1947.

Plate 1:— The old and the new — road vehicles at Paddington on 9 September 1943 showing *left* Scammell 3 wheel tractor and trailer, *middle* A pair horse wagon with Carter Smith in the chair and *right* A Bedford 4 wheel tractor and trailer.

Horse Drawn Vehicles

The Railway Horse

The introduction of steam traction led people to suppose that the services of the horse would be rendered unnecessary or at any rate greatly restricted, but this was not so, as in 1909 the Great Western Railway had over 3000 horses.

The actual number on stud on 31 December 1926 was 2828 compared with 2896 in the previous year. In 1936 the number was down to 2000 and at the end of 1936 it was 1773. Out of this total 500 were employed in London. Just after the Second World War the total was almost 1000. Surprisingly the last cartage horse at Paddington left the service as late as 1954.

The average price paid for a horse, in 1926, was £44 and its life was about 7yrs 3 months.

Great thought was given to their feeding and stabling. The Company maintained an immense provender store at Didcot and a Home of Rest was established at West Ealing.

In London a large three floored building was maintained at South Wharf Road, near Paddington, known as the Mint Stables which included a farrier's shop. Horses had to be shod quite often, a set of shoes lasting about a month.

Plate 2:— The Horse Hospital at West Ealing in 1909. This Home of Rest adjoined the Great Western Athletic Ground. In the winter 24 horses could be tended in stables, and in summer 40 could be dealt with. Note the two wheeled water carrier in the foreground, built at Swindon. Not all tenders were metal!

Plate 3:— Single horse drawn light spring cart No. 1288. Built Swindon Works. Photograph taken in 1890. Company initials and number are stamped on shaft.

Plate 4:— Single horse drawn parcels van No. 143. Built Swindon Works. Photograph taken 1890.

Plate 5:— Single horse drawn omnibus. Date built not known but photographed at Swindon Works in May 1894. It is apparent that this vehicle was preserved for a period of time A very simple garter surrounding two crests adorns the side below the lettering. Fitted with foot brake.

Plate 6:— I.K. Brunel's horse drawn Britzska "Galloper" nicknamed the "Flying Hearse". Contemporary reports state that this vehicle was drawn by either a four horse or two horse team. Specially built to accommodate "himself" his plans and cigar boxes. Completely or partly built by the G.W.R. Company; notice the initials stamped on the wheel bosses. Fitted with a hand brake. Photograph taken in May 1894; another example of temporary preservation. It is apparent that the livery was somewhat special with gold leaf shaded lettering.

6

Plate 7:— Single horse drawn wagon No. 2401. Tare weight 1-1-3, built Swindon Works. Photographed in Jan. 1900. Fitted with foot brake. The chain apparatus hanging on the side is a skid for placing under rear wheel when the vehicle is stationary. Note the luxury seating arrangement complete with facility for holding the whip. Most horse drawn vehicles were allocated to a particular station and were branded accordingly.

Plate 8:— Single horse drawn wagon No. 100. Tare weight under 1 ton. Built Swindon Works. Photographed 11 January 1905. Fitted with foot brake, very similar design to vehicle No. 2401 but with minor differences. The plate on the side states that the load is not to exceed 2 tons — quite a load for one horse. The official recognised load, in the London area, for a powerful horse was 30-35 cwts and 3 tons 10 cwts for a pair.

G.W.R.— Single Horse Drawn Passenger Parcels Van

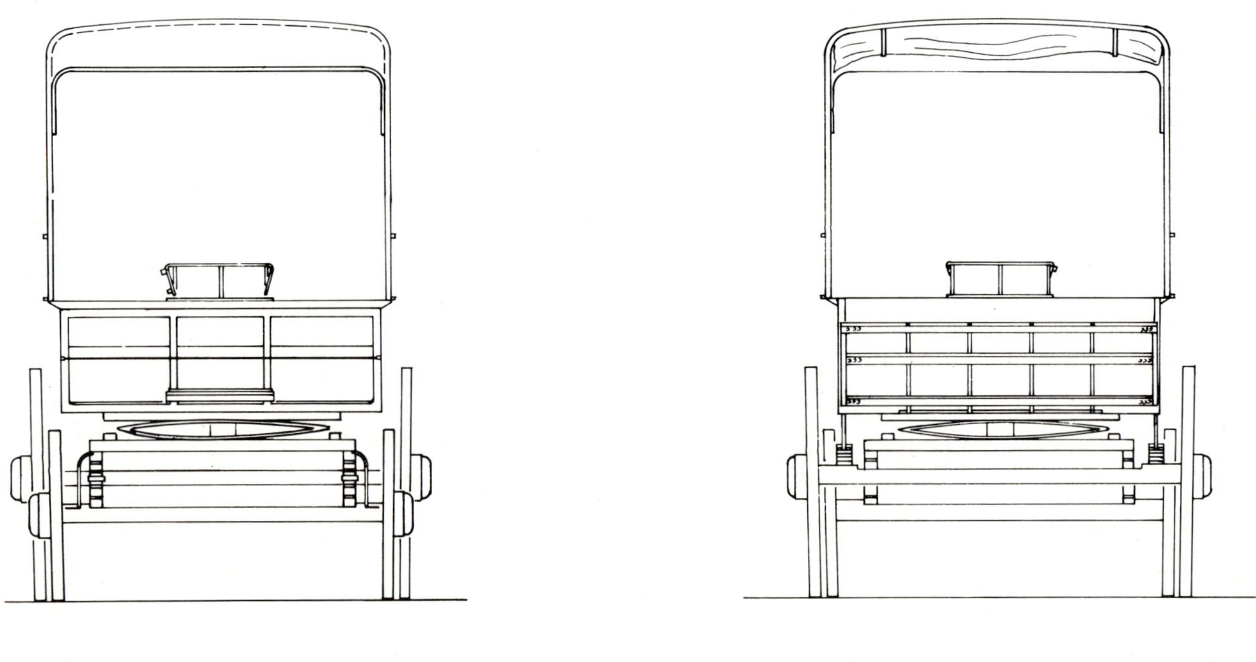

Scale 7mm/1ft

FEET

Plate 9:— Single horse drawn passenger train parcels van No. 231. Tare weight 0-14-2. Built Swindon works. Photographed in February 1900. Fitted with foot brake. G.W.R. stamped on brass wheel bosses and on inside of felloes.

Plate 10:— Single horse drawn passenger train parcels van No. 232. Tare weight 0-14-0 (written on the negative but not on vehicle.) This Van and the one above were based at Bristol.

Plate 11:—Single horse drawn parcels van No. 243, used for deliveries in the Henley-on-Thames area. Tare weight 0-7-3. Built Swindon works. Photographed in February 1900. Fitted with handbrake. G.W.R. stamped on brass wheel bosses as with most Swindon productions.

Plate 12:— Pair horse drawn passenger train parcels delivery van No. 166.P. Tare weight 1-1-0. Built Swindon Works. Photographed in May 1902. Fitted with foot brake. Underneath the van, resting on the axles, is the perch to which the two horses were attached when in its normal position. ►

Plate 13:— Single horse drawn express parcel van No. 305. Built Swindon Works. Photographed on 6 May 1908. Fitted with Foot Brake. Note windows in side of tilt. Turning circle does not appear to be very great. ►

GREAT WESTERN RAILWAY
DELIVERY VAN
FOR
PASSENGER TRAIN PARCELS.
GREAT WESTERN RAILWAY PARCEL VAN
166.P. PADDINGTON STATION

GREAT WESTERN
RAILWAY
EXPRESS
PARCELS
SERVICES
ADDISON ROAD STATION
305

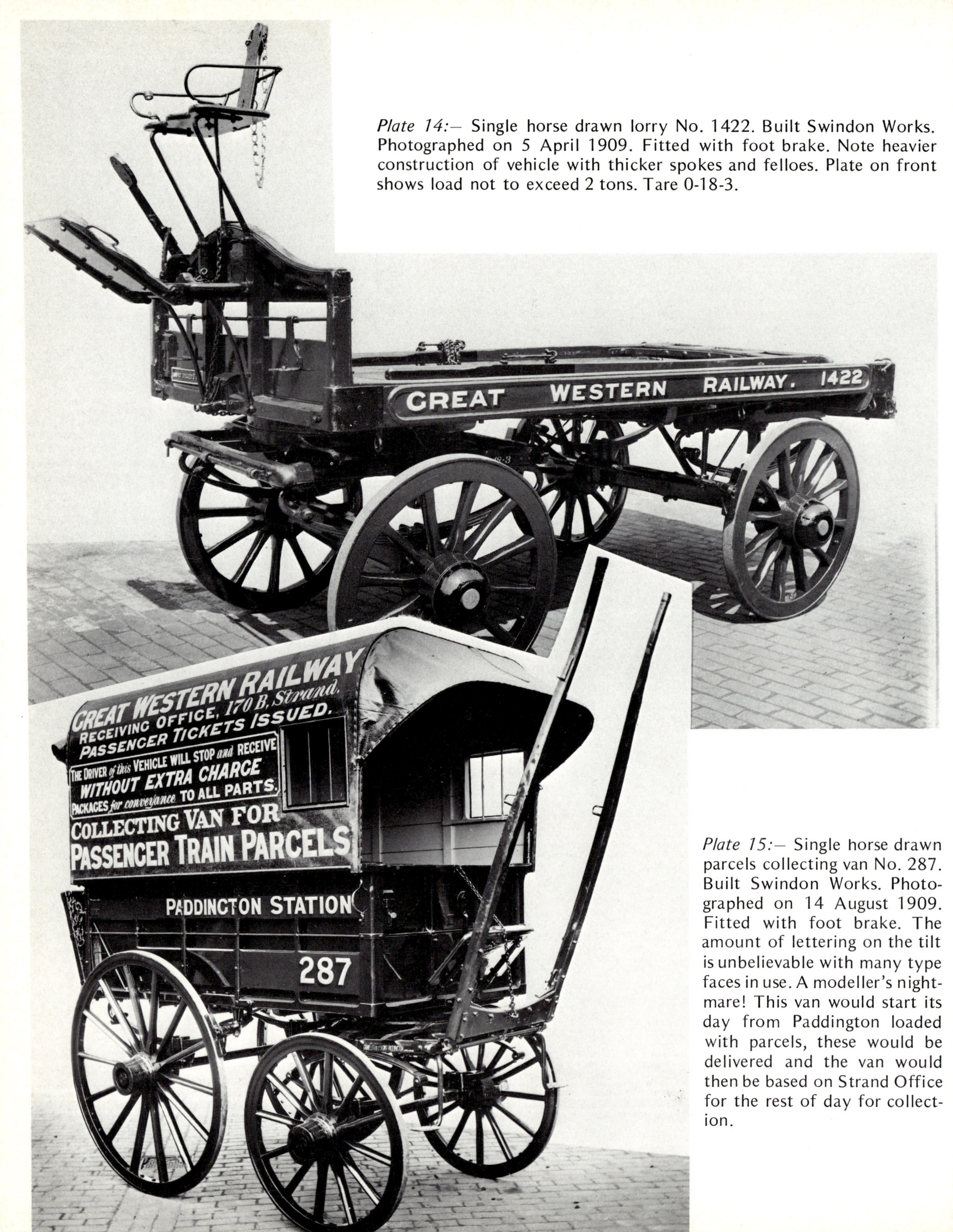

Plate 14:— Single horse drawn lorry No. 1422. Built Swindon Works. Photographed on 5 April 1909. Fitted with foot brake. Note heavier construction of vehicle with thicker spokes and felloes. Plate on front shows load not to exceed 2 tons. Tare 0-18-3.

Plate 15:— Single horse drawn parcels collecting van No. 287. Built Swindon Works. Photographed on 14 August 1909. Fitted with foot brake. The amount of lettering on the tilt is unbelievable with many type faces in use. A modeller's nightmare! This van would start its day from Paddington loaded with parcels, these would be delivered and the van would then be based on Strand Office for the rest of day for collection.

Plate 16:— Three horse team with wagon No. 532. Built Swindon Works. Photographed in 1909. It was basically designed to be hauled by two horses but, when required due to hilly conditions or heavy loads, an additional horse (chain horse) was attached. Foot brake fitted and applied fully. Hoops and tarpaulin fitted. Note carter's apron.

Plate 17:— Four horse team with wagon No. 546. Built Swindon Works. Photographed in 1909. This vehicle was fitted with two single horse shafts and obviously additional chain horses were needed because of the load. One hopes that the goods were loaded systematically and that the first item to be delivered wasn't at the bottom. Notice the carter had a plank as a seat unlike the other picture on this page. Vehicle fitted with screw type brake worked from the side of lorry.

Plate 18:— Pair horse drawn delivery wagon No. 535. Built Swindon Works. Photographed in May 1937 at Paddington. Fitted with hoops, tarpaulin, also foot brake, which is fully applied. Note fancy whip handle complete with bow. Carter Smith is in the chair again. The chain was used for locking rear wheels when stationary. The advertisement is very interesting — cigarettes were 10 for 4d (2p).

Plate 19:— Single horse drawn lorry No. 4081. Built Swindon Works. Photographed on 9 July 1941. Fitted with foot brake, not complete, no seat fitted. Tare 0-17-0. Load not to exceed 2 tons. Edge of shafts and wheel bosses painted white to facilitate visibility in blackout during the Second World War.

Plate 20:— Single horse drawn parcels van No. 4901. The ultimate in horse drawn vehicle design, photographed on 3 October 1937. This vehicle was experimentally introduced in Oxford. It had several modern features including ball-bearing axle boxes, pneumatic tyres and electric lighting. Hub brakes were installed, similar to motor car practice, instead of a primitive shoe working on exterior of iron tyre. The driver's seat was recessed and protected from weather by projecting canopy and scuttle dash at front. Tare 16-3-16.

Plate 21:— Single horse drawn parcels van No. 4902 in a square near Paddington Station in April 1938. Parcel carter Mr. T. Hoare with this turn-out won first prize in the London van horse parade in Regent's Park on Easter Monday 1938. Mr. Hoare also received the R.S.P.C.A. medal for the best undocked horse in the parade.

Plate 22:— Road wagon ship (Wheel Section) Swindon Works on 16 January 1915. This shop was built on the site of the original wagon shop. The importance of such a depot can be realised when at this date there were upwards of 3,600 horse drawn road vehicles in use. The G.W.R. adopted the "Artillery" pattern wheel because of its strength and it proved ideal. This particular type of wheel had extra spokes and was developed by the Army, as should one or two spokes be shot away during battle conditions the wheel would still remain sound.

    Plate 23:— Road wagon shop — Swindon Works — 31 July 1907.

Plate 24:— This 9 h.p. G.W.R. team is moving a 17½ ton Burrell showman's engine from the Agricultural Hall to Paddington for conveyance to Plymouth on 30 January 1922. This showman's engine was built by Charles Burrell & Sons Ltd in 1922, works no. 3912. It was an 8n.h.p. D.C.C. engine built for Anderton & Rowland. This engine is preserved by a Mr. W.G. Chamberlain of Peterborough and now has 'Pride of the Fens' written along the sides.

Mechanical Cartage Vehicles

The Great Western Railway first entered the mechanical commercial vehicle era in 1902 with a Thornycroft steam wagon. This started a partnership between the two companies which lasted up to Nationalisation and beyond. After the initial steam wagon there followed two Milnes Daimler lorries and two Wallis Stevens steam tractors in 1904/5. Other types were added and according to an official G.W.R. report of 1909 the goods and parcels service was operated by the following mechanically propelled vehicles, supporting the horse drawn types:—

Birkenhead	*1 steam wagon, 3 motor parcel vans*
Paddington Goods	*2 petrol lorries, 2 electric vehicles*
Bilston Goods	*2 steam traction engines*
Slough Goods	*1 petrol lorry*
Saltash & Callington	*1 petrol lorry*
Cardiff	*2 motor parcel vans*
Birmingham	*3 motor parcel vans*

An experimental electric vehicle was introduced in 1906 and another type built at Slough in 1908.

In 1910 a total of 25 mechanical cartage vehicles were in service. The Straker Squire 12h.p. vans added in 1909 were built to the design and specification of the Great Western Railway. 1914 saw the start of the bulk orders from John I Thornycroft & Co. Ltd.

The first World War encouraged the use of mechanical transport and in 1919 surplus army vehicles were dumped at Slough Trading Estate. The Great Western purchased 130 A.E.C. 3½ ton lorries out of this collection, which were somewhat reconstructed with interchangeable bodies in order that they could serve as charabancs in Summer and as goods vehicles in Winter.

Further electric vehicles of a different type entered service in 1919.

In 1924 the G.W.R. inaugurated contract hire by which vans were placed at the exclusive use of any company that required them, and were painted in their own liveries. On 4 January 1926 MacFarlane, Lang & Co entered into such a contract with the G.W.R.

Due to the enormous increase in the numbers of road vehicles used by the G.W.R. more accommodation for the repair of them became necessary. The Road Transport Department at Slough, originally set up in 1905, built a new brick structure in 1926.

Many vehicles of a special type were introduced to cater for very diverse forms of traffic like the large 10 ton six-wheeled Thornycrofts for sand and gravel cartage at Theale. Here, like the majority of vehicles, the chassis was purchased from the manufacturers and the body was built by the G.W.R.

Foden Steam Wagons were purchased in 1929 for heavy cartage work.

September 1931 saw the introduction of the now familiar articulated vehicles (apart from an experimental type in 1918). These virtually sounded the death knell of the horse-drawn types and by January 1937 there were 333 three ton three-wheelers, 194 six ton three-wheelers and 49 six ton four-wheelers.

The Great Western Railway's authorised cartage equipment on 31 December 1936 comprised the following:—

Mechanised units	2328
Trailers	1589
Horses	1773

The consumption of petrol in the same year was approximately 2,177,500 gallons.

The London Parcels Cartage Service based on Paddington in 1938 consisted of 96 motors, varying in capacity from 1 ton to 8 tons. The total normal mileage was 3,400 miles daily, 132 regular rounds being operated, of which 123 were by motor and the remainder by horse. A good average day's traffic was 37,000 parcels. In 1930 the cartage staff numbered 112 and the number of parcels dealt with was 6,873,000. In 1938 there were 136 vanmen and 10,170,000 parcels.

Figures like these give some idea of the size of the Company's fleet.

A certain amount of Parliamentary legislation affected the running of the road motor fleet in the 1930's such as the Road Traffic Act 1930 which had important provisions regarding hours of staff, weights, speed and third party insurance.

The Road and Rail Traffic Act 1933 embodied a scheme for licensing commercial road vehicles *(1) Public Carriers Licence 'A' (2) Limited Carriers Licence 'B' (3) Private Carriers Licence 'C'.*

The Finance Act 1933 entirely reorganised the scale of taxation for motor vehicles, which added about £30,000 a year to the G.W.R.'s road vehicle expenses. Alterations were necessary in the way of lightening vehicles to bring them within the lower category for licensing. This was done by replacing solid rubber tyres with pneumatics and getting rid of trailers not fitted with rubber tyres.

During 1936 it became necessary for any person who was not in the possession of a driver's licence before 1 April 1934 to take a test. A further condition demanded that those drivers who handled certain cars classified as heavy goods vehicles, and who had not driven such vehicles for a qualifying period, had to be examined. Employers of more than 250 drivers of mechanically propelled vehicles could appoint their own examiners. A new school for this purpose was established at Taplow in 1939.

As from 1 January 1937 it became compulsory for all windscreens to consist of safety glass.

Speedometers became compulsory on vehicles placed in service on and after 1st October 1937. Special plates were to be carried from this date by vehicles limited to a legal speed of 20 mph and by trailers.

The following pages and photographs will tell more conclusively the story of the Great Western's enterprise in the road cartage business.

Plate 26:— A view of A.7645 this time loaded with fish boxes. One can imagine this primitive vehicle with low bonnet and oil lamps on this journey between Paddington and Billingsgate, a regular run, rattling over the cobbled streets up to an unofficial 20m.p.h. For this traffic the lorry was fitted with special sides. The actual fleet number of this vehicle was thought to have been 37 but as can be seen the registration number was used.

Plate 25:— Milnes Daimler 20h.p. goods lorry No.A.7645, one of the type introduced in 1904. Notice the simple steel chassis with horse drawn vehicle type decking. The wheels look anything but round and have iron tyres; the lever handbrake acted on the outside of the wheels. The cupboard under the bench seat probably contained tools, ropes and even the Carman's lunch. The driver was his own mechanic, a half day every week being devoted to overhaul and adjustments. Most uniforms were of leather, complete with gaiters and this was the only protection from the weather. The load looks very insecure and does not appear to be roped.

Plate 27:— Milnes Daimler 30h.p. goods lorry at Penzance (date not known but almost certainly 1905.) Judging by the interest shown by both the bowler hatted and other staff, the vehicle had only just been delivered and was fairly new. Plymouth Registration. Wheels still have iron tyres also the very railway looking type screw brake was fitted in addition to hand brake.

Plate 28:— This superb photograph shows the first motor parcels van in service on the G.W.R. It was built by the Wolseley Tool & Motor Car Co. Ltd., of Birmingham, and is depicted here in one of the many squares near Paddington Station in 1905. This vehicle had chain drive and the wheels were fitted with solid rubber tyres, single at the front, double at the back. The gold leaf shaded lettering is an excellent example of the signwriter's art. The Carman appears to be in an ordinary suit.

Plate 29:— In 1906 an experimental electric delivery vehicle was put into service by the G.W.R. on the recommendation of the Chief Goods Manager, after his visit to the U.S.A., where a similar vehicle was seen in use. It was of 2 tons capacity and was propelled by two enclosed electric motors working on a current of 80 volts. This picture shows No. 95, a new type electric lorry for parcels and goods delivery work, in service at Paddington on 8 June 1908. It was built at the Motor Car Department workshops at Slough and is a development from the original prototype of 1906 with many improvements. The vehicle was driven by a 40 cell battery giving it a capacity of about 30 miles on one charge. Note the caliper brakes working on the motor shaft. The wheels have four inch thick solid rubber tyres.

GreatWesternRailway
PARCEL VAN.
LC-1083

GREAT WESTERN RAILWAY
PADDINGTON
STATION.
95

Plate 30:— This vehicle No. 109 was officially known as a motor parcel cart and it entered service in 1910. The chassis was built by Sidney Straker & Squire Ltd. of London with the body manufactured at Swindon Works, where the photograph was taken on 23 November 1909. Six were put to work in the Birkenhead area. The Vans were fitted with 2cyl. vertical engines developing 14h.p. and designed to carry 15 cwt. Speed was 15m.p.h. The Carman was afforded better weather protection with front screen and canopy. Wheels fitted with Dunlop solid rubber tyres.

Plate 31:— A nearside view of a similar vehicle to that above. This time without Carman, oil lamps and horn. Notice the silencer runs across the vehicle instead of in line.

Plate 32 and *Plate 33*:— During 1919 the G.W.R. put into service further types of electric vehicles for goods and cartage work. In order to obtain information of actual working of electric propulsion the Company purchased the following:—

Four 5 ton for goods, built by General Vehicle Co., Tyseley, Birmingham.

Two 3½ ton for parcels
Four 2½ ton for parcels }built by Ransomes, Sims & Jefferies Ltd of Ipswich.
One 1½ ton for parcels

The photographs show three of the 2½ ton Orwell electric parcel vans Nos. E 11, E 12, E 14 at Paddington. The driver's cab was a standard type for electric vehicles and was designed by the G.W.R. Motor Car Dept. It afforded good protection for the driver without restricting his vision. These cabs were fixed to the chassis. The load carrying bodies built at Swindon were easily removable. The paint date on all three was 24 March 1919. The livery appears to be crimson lake with garter Coat of Arms (with crest either side) on cab side and shaded G.W.R. lettering in front. Black tilt with white letters. On the frontal view vehicle E.14 has rear mudguards whereas the others have not. As can be seen, two traction motors drove the front wheels and naturally the vans had electric lights. The speed was 9 — 14 m.p.h.

Plate 34:— Offside view of 2½ ton Orwell electric parcels van No. E 14. In this view one can see the Ransomes works plate No. 1068. No electric lamps are fitted. Load not to exceed 2 tons 10 cwt. This photograph taken at Swindon on 3 July 1919.

Plate 36 and Plate 37:— A.E.C. 3½ ton lorry No. 644 photographed in the early 1920's. These were ex-Army vehicles purchased second-hand after the first World War; a total of about 130 were acquired. The flat body and cab were manufactured by the G.W.R. Although a very reliable vehicle one couldn't possibly call it handsome. These lorries proved, when fitted with special sides, the most suitable for the cartage of sugar beet. This chassis was one of those used with charabanc bodies in summer and reverted to goods work in the winter. It can be seen that the chassis has been recently repainted but the body has not.

Plate 35:— A fine example of the then Road Motor Constructor's art, a 1 ton parcel van No. 527 based on a 30 cwt chassis supplied by H.G. Burford & Co. Ltd., of North Kensington, London. The 10 cwt body built at Swindon works. Photograph taken at Westbourne Park on 17 October 1922. Fourteen of this type had been built by this time. The body portion was constructed of timber, the tilt being made of light match-boarding covered in canvas. Wings over the solid rubber tyred wheels had combined running board at front. In this instance the tilt was painted cream with main body chocolate brown. Lettering appears to be brown also.

Plate 38:— Another view of an A.E.C. 3½ ton lorry, No. 801 photographed on 28 September 1921. The Swindon paint date was 18 September 1921. In this case the body had sides and was fitted with a canvas tilt. These vehicles had 45 bhp engines and the gear boxes had 4 forward speeds and reverse. A contemporary advertisement by the Associated Equipment Co. Ltd. stated that these vehicles when new cost £1075 and that 10,000 had been supplied to the War Department. The Walthamstow Factory produced one chassis every half hour.

Plate 39:— A line-up of seven A.E.C. 3½ ton lorries shortly after delivery probably in 1921.

Plate 40:— 30 cwt. parcel van No 950. Shown on this page and the next is one of the nicest looking motor vans produced in the 1920's. The 30 cwt A.1. chassis was supplied by John I. Thornycroft & Co. Ltd of Basingstoke. The body was built at Swindon works. The photographs were taken on 25 March 1926, the paint date being 6 March 1926. The wheels were still fitted with solid rubber tyres. The front wings, however, were beginning to be moulded instead of the plain flat type. Oil lamps for side lighting only. Speed 12 mph — quite fast enough after dark! The driver was provided with cushions — quite a luxury after the hard seats of previous types.

Plate 41:— Thornycroft 30 cwt parcel van No. 950 (*Nearside view*)

Plate 42:— Thornycroft 30 cwt flat lorry No. 947. The same A.1. chassis but with flat body built at Swindon Works in 1926. Photograph taken on 25 March 1926. Body was fitted with brackets along the sides for the iron hoops to slot into. The rolled tarpaulin on the cab roof was placed over the hoops — quite an experience in gale force winds! A fire extinguisher was fitted in the cab.

G.W.R.— Thornycroft A1 Motor Parcels Van

Scale 7mm/1ft

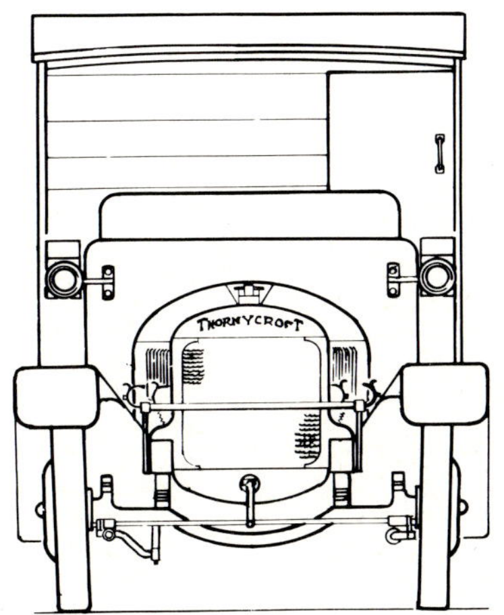

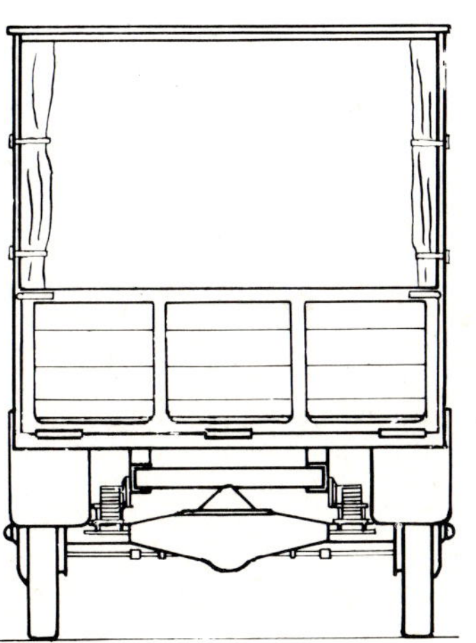

FEET

Plate 43:— The difference in time between this photograph and those on the previous pages is 18 months. This 30 cwt Thornycroft parcels van No. 981 on A.1. chassis was photographed at Swindon Works on 5 October 1927. It is almost identical to No. 950. The major improvement is the provision of Dunlop pneumatic tyres and in consequence the driver loses his soft cushions. Another development is the fitting of electric head and side lamps. Brackets were still provided for oil lamps, however, as the Great Western always believed in wearing both belt and braces! The line of the roof was slightly more curved over the cab area giving even more protection from the weather.

Plate 44 and *Plate 45:*— A superlative Great Western / Thornycroft combination. Photographs taken in the late 1920's. This 30 cwt van with A.1. chassis, was probably one of the large number ordered for the Railhead schemes started in 1928. Main differences were doors fitted to side of cab, windscreen installed and side and rear oil lamps electrified. Speed uprated to 20 m.p.h. Body No G 1500, chassis bears number 2000 which was to be the new fleet number later.

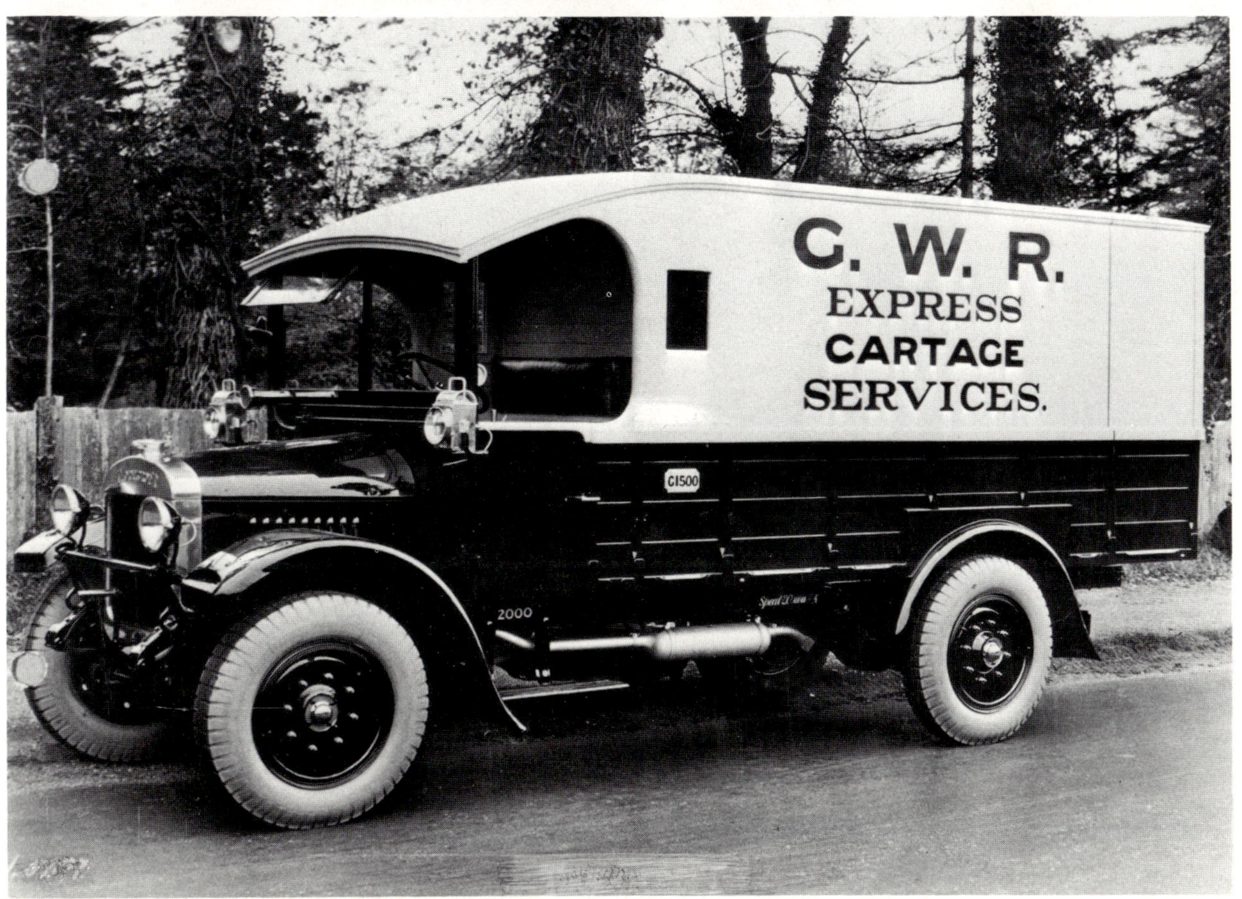

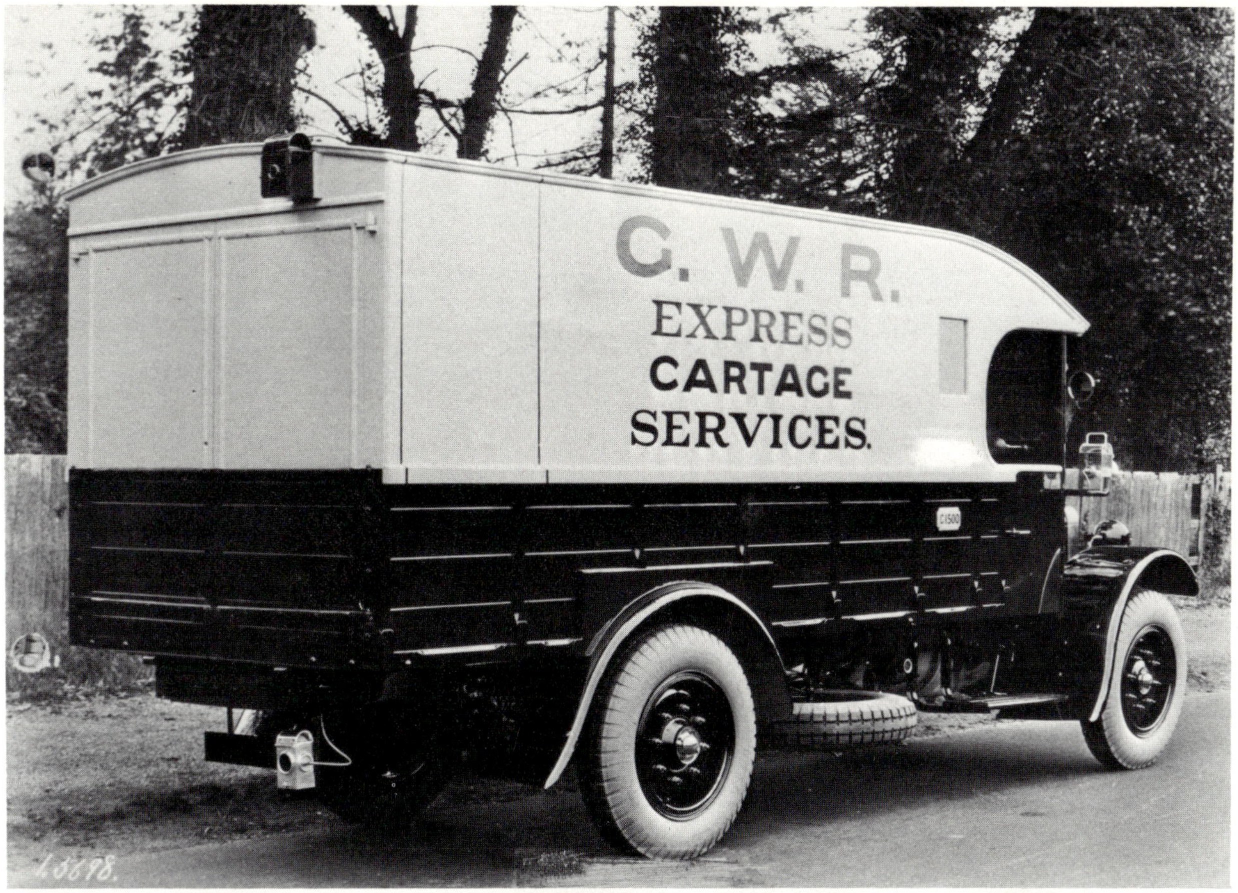
G. W. R.
EXPRESS
CARTAGE
SERVICES.
G1500

G. W. R.
EXPRESS
CARTAGE
SERVICES.
G1500
2000

Plate 46:— A versatile group of Thornycroft vans and two Burford vehicles (extreme left) at Cardiff on 30 July 1930. This array was part of the Co-ordinated Transport Service in the Cardiff area, started by the G.W.R. in 1928. Known as the 'Railhead' delivery service, by which the whole responsibility of consignments, including unpacking, collection and crediting of empties etc., was undertaken by the staff at the railhead centre on behalf of the customer. Among the vehicles in the photograph are one or two on contract hire, such as MacFarlane, Lang & Co.

Plate 47:— 4 Ton 45h.p. Thornycroft road motor lorry No. 1307 fitted with high sided body built at Swindon Works, and hoops provided to support tarpaulin when required. Fitted with solid rubber tyred wheels and electric headlamps plus brackets for oil lamps. Major difference was the forward control system of steering which enabled the driver to be positioned further forward beside the engine, thereby giving more room for loads on the same chassis.

Plate 48:— No. 578 a 30 cwt Burford forward control chassis fitted with Swindon parcels van body. Photographed on 25 March 1926. The protective tarpaulin makes the driver look as though he has retired for the night. The wheel design is interesting as it appears to be a compromise between the old horse-drawn wagon type and the new style motor vehicle variety.

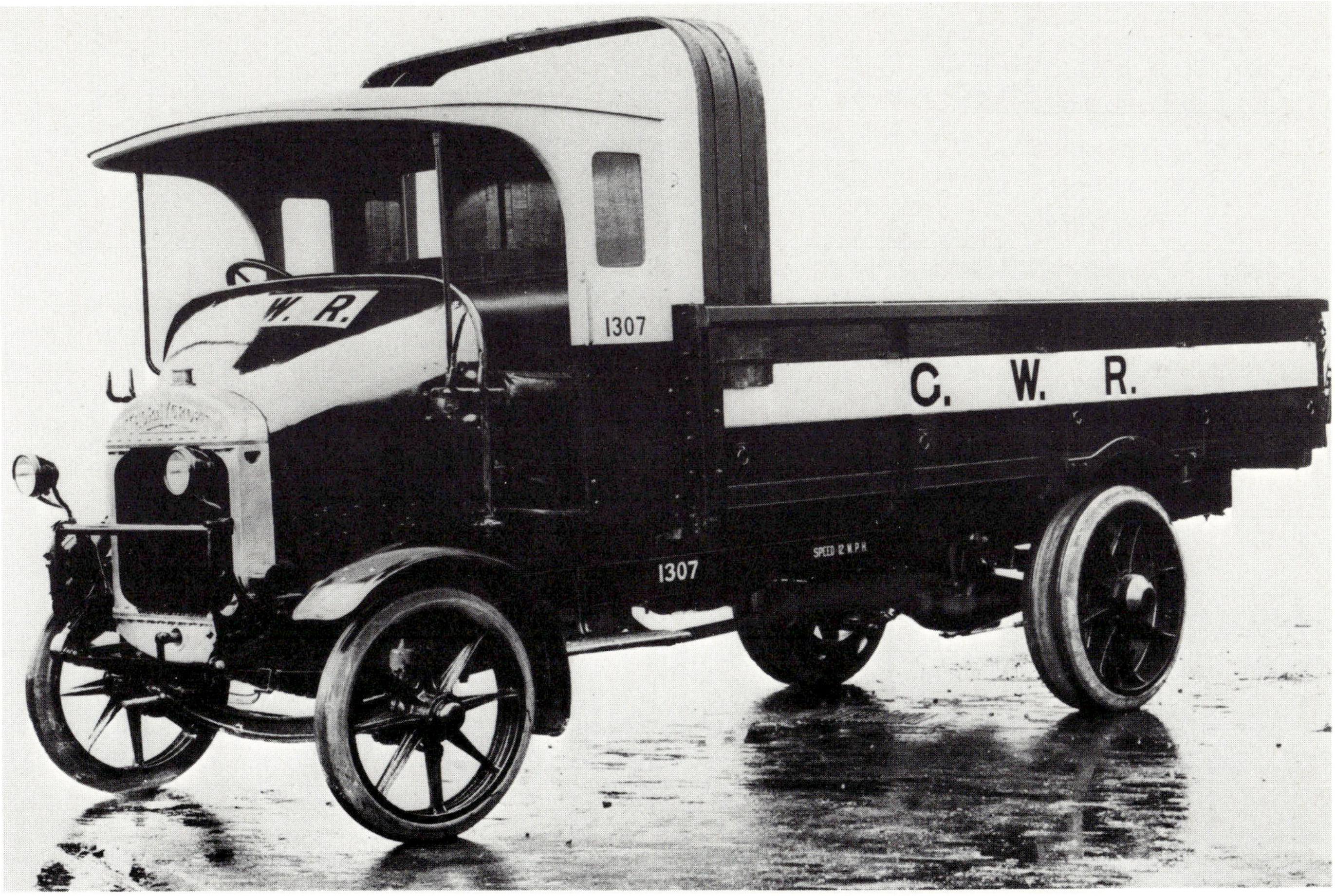
W. R.
1307
G. W. R.
1307
SPEED 12 M.P.H.

G. W. R.
EXPRESS
CARTAGE
SERVICES
"HOLIDAY HAUNTS"
6D
578
G.W.R
XP 7602

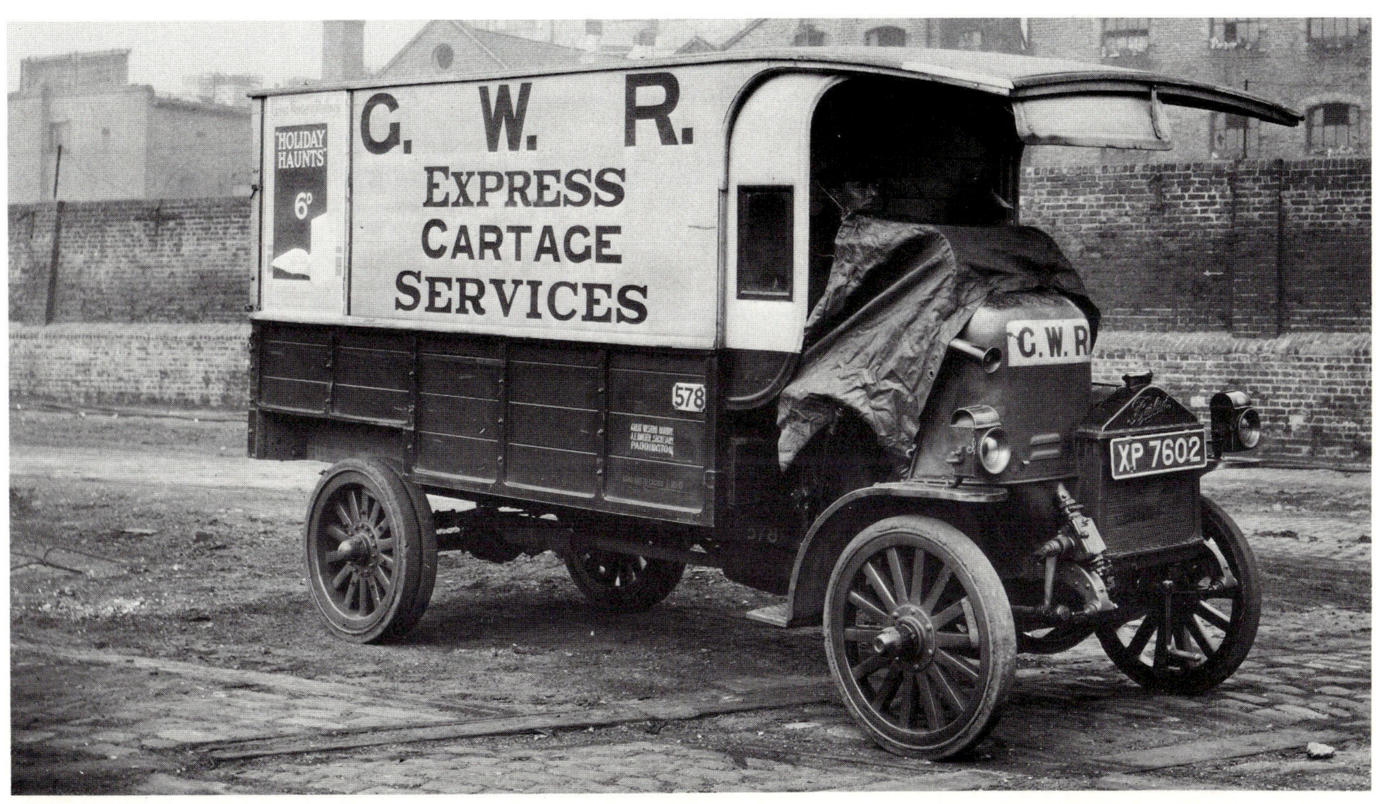

Plate 49:— A view taken in the corner of the inwards shed at Birmingham (Hockley) Goods Yard during April 1927. A forward control 30 cwt Burford flat bodied lorry No. 546 is shown in the foreground and beyond are a 4 ton Thornycroft, a 3½ ton A.E.C. and another 4 ton Thornycroft.

Road Motor Department — Repair Shops — Slough

The repair shops were originally set up in 1905 but due to the increase in the fleet of motors it became apparent that the existing accommodation was not sufficient. In 1926 a new brick structure was erected close to the old premises, it was 228ft long by 81ft wide, with additional smaller bays to accommodate the smithy and engine testing apparatus. All the work was done under one roof, from the initial stripping down and cleaning to the final painting and varnishing. For the latter operations an area was totally screened off to exclude dust. A number of additional machines were installed, the most important being a cylinder grinder, which was capable of reboring the cylinders of any vehicle used by the G.W.R. Another new machine was a vulcanising plant for repairing damaged pneumatic tyres. The most interesting innovation was the lifting gantries, made at Slough, which were built to bridge any vehicle and were used for slinging heavy components, such as engines, in and out of the chassis. These gantries could be moved either in a longitudinal or lateral direction and even slewed round.

Plate 50 and Plate 51: — As described on the previous page, the Road Motor Department Repair Shops at Slough as they looked in April 1927. The top photograph shows the exterior of shops and new office block, with the running shed in the distance. Lower picture gives an idea of the repair shop interior.

Plate 52 and Plate 53:— 4 ton Thornycroft forward control chassis fitted with sliding tilt supplied by the Portsmouth Motor Company. This vehicle No. 1334 was photographed on 26 May 1927 at a depot thought to be Park Royal. The tilt was constructed to enable the driver or loading staff to slide it forward so as to leave three-quarters of the loading space open. When closed complete weather protection was provided. Quite a number of vehicles were fitted in this way.

Plate 54:– Another version of a 30 cwt A.1. chassis Thornycroft van adapted for contract hire. This vehicle No. 976 had a body built at Swindon. As previously stated, the G.W.R. entered into a contract with MacFarlane, Lang & Co. in 1926. This photograph was taken at Redruth in January 1928. It appears that the firm's nameboard was interchangeable and could be fixed to any suitable vehicle. Other points of interest are full windscreen fitted and roof rack for biscuit tins. The cushion for the driver is reinstated even though the van is fitted with pneumatic tyres. Electric head and side lamps, also oil for standby. Speed 12 mph. Vehicle bore standard G.W.R. livery and lettering.

Plate 55:– 4 ton Thornycroft van No. 1347 with solid tyres and electric headlamps. Full windscreen fitted. Vehicle on contract hire to The India & China Tea Co. and bears their livery. Body built at Swindon and photographed on 10 November 1927.

G.W.R.— Thornycroft Forward Control A1 Motor Lorry

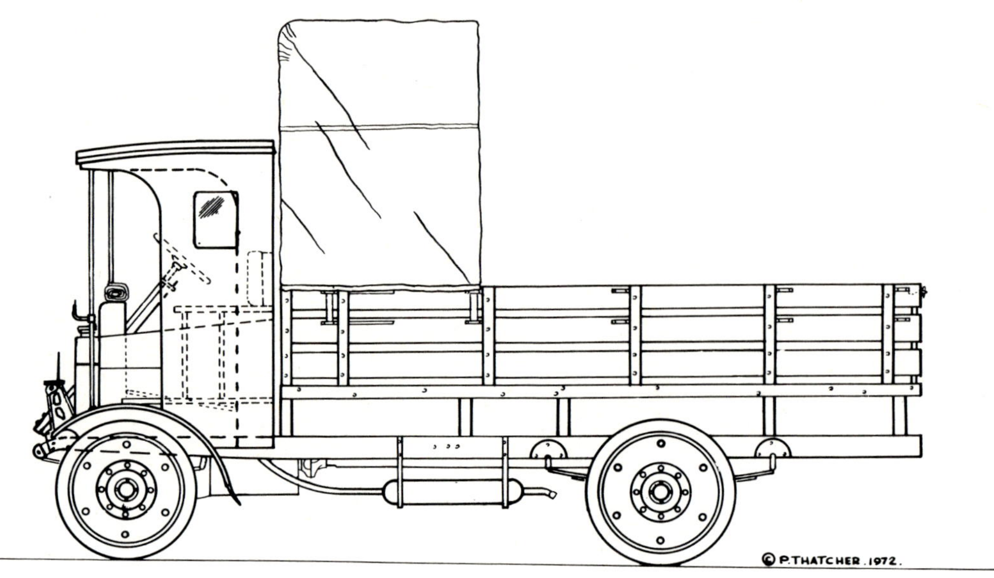

Scale 7mm/1ft

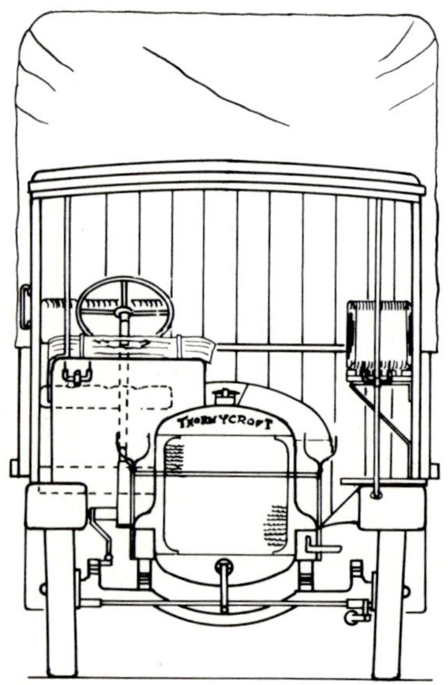

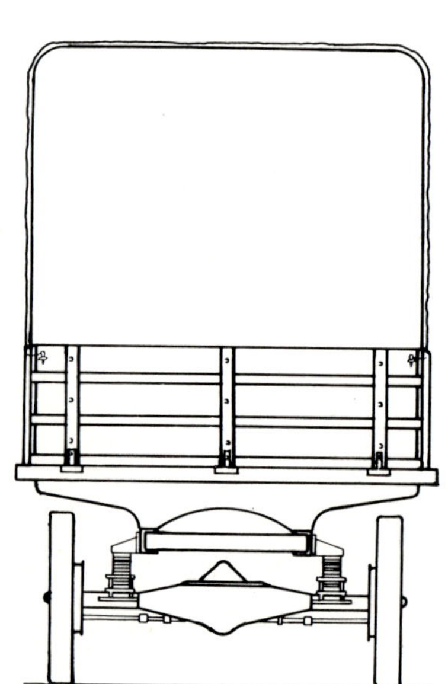

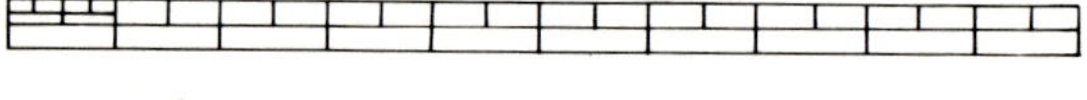

FEET

Plate 56 and *Plate 57:—* Two views of a 30 cwt. Thornycroft forward control chassis fitted with flat body, sides and brackets in use with hoops and partial tarpaulin. This vehicle numbered 1445, bearing Swindon paint date 22 June 1928, was photographed at the Westbourne Park Road Motor Depot on 19 October 1928. The lever just in front of the rear wheels is presumably the device for anchoring the body to the chassis. Most bodies were removable for obvious reasons of maintenance. To the left of the top picture a flat body is shown on trestles. Of interest in the bottom photograph is the heap of discarded solid rubber tyres.

Plate 58:— A very nice lightweight motor parcels van No. 1122, chassis built by Morris Commercial Cars Ltd, Birmingham. Body partly built at Swindon Works. Photograph taken about the year 1928. Fitted with electric head and side lamps, pneumatic tyres and full windscreen. It appears that the G.W.R. thought this vehicle's electric lamps were completely reliable as there was no provision for fixing oil lamps.

Plate 59:— 4 ton Thornycroft forward control road motor lorry No.1323. Photograph taken in Chiseldon Goods Yard on 15 June 1928 during the unloading of Stanton pipes for the Swindon water pipe line. The rail mounted crane in the roadway is of particular interest.

Plate 60:— 30 cwt. Thornycroft forward control chassis fitted with Swindon flat body. No. 1857 is shown as running in October 1930. The "M" on the top of the cab is thought to denote that the vehicle belonged to the maintenance department. Swindon paint date was 31 May 1929. A very primitive looking lorry considering the date, with no electric light and no windscreen. Instead of the usual 'Dunlop' tyres this vehicle and that on page 39 were fitted with solid 'Henley Air Cushion' tyres. The G.W.R. plate fitted to the bonnet was becoming standard at this time. The signwriter evidently considered there was not room for the full word "Railway", as on some of the horse drawn vehicles.

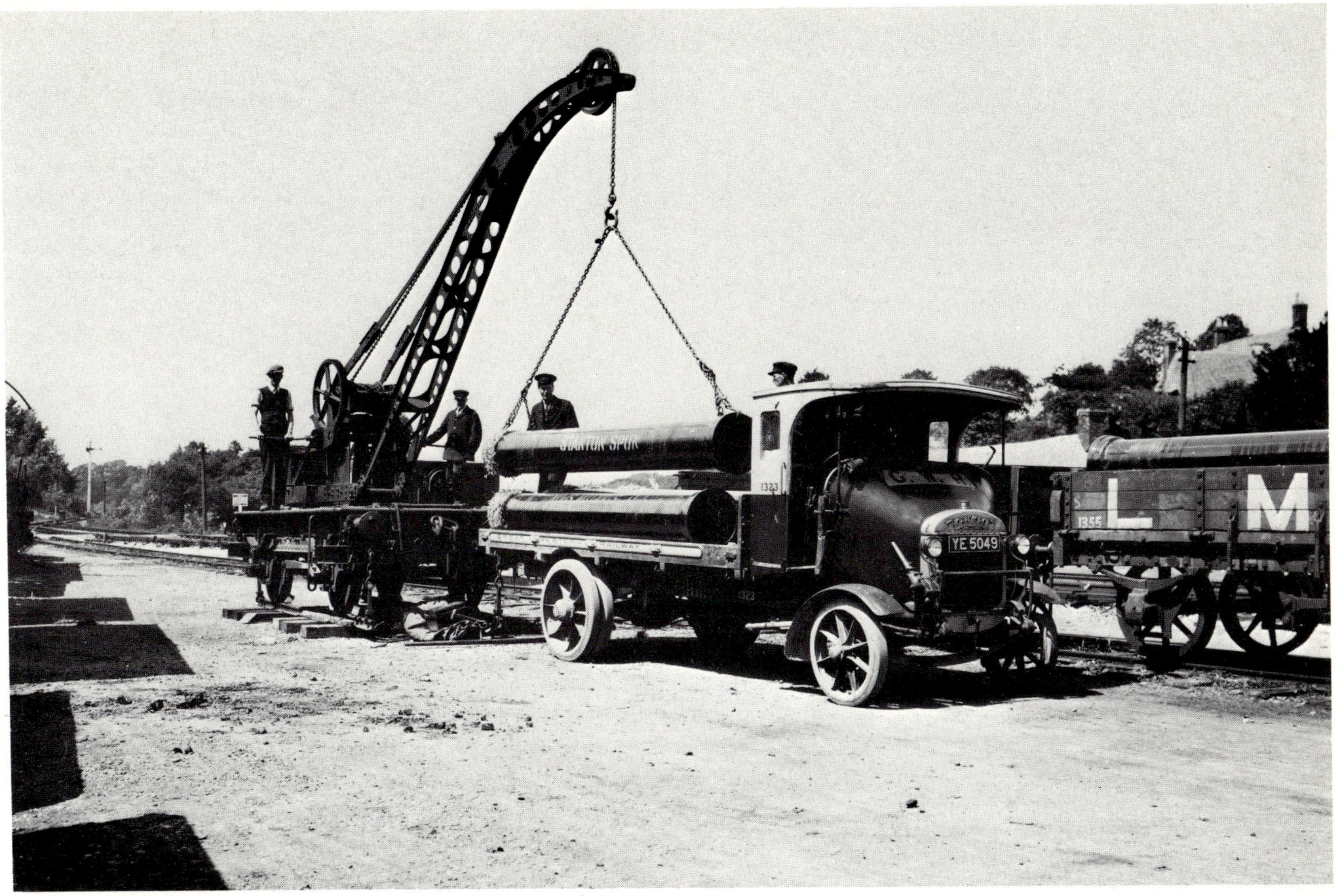
YE 5049
L M
1355
1323

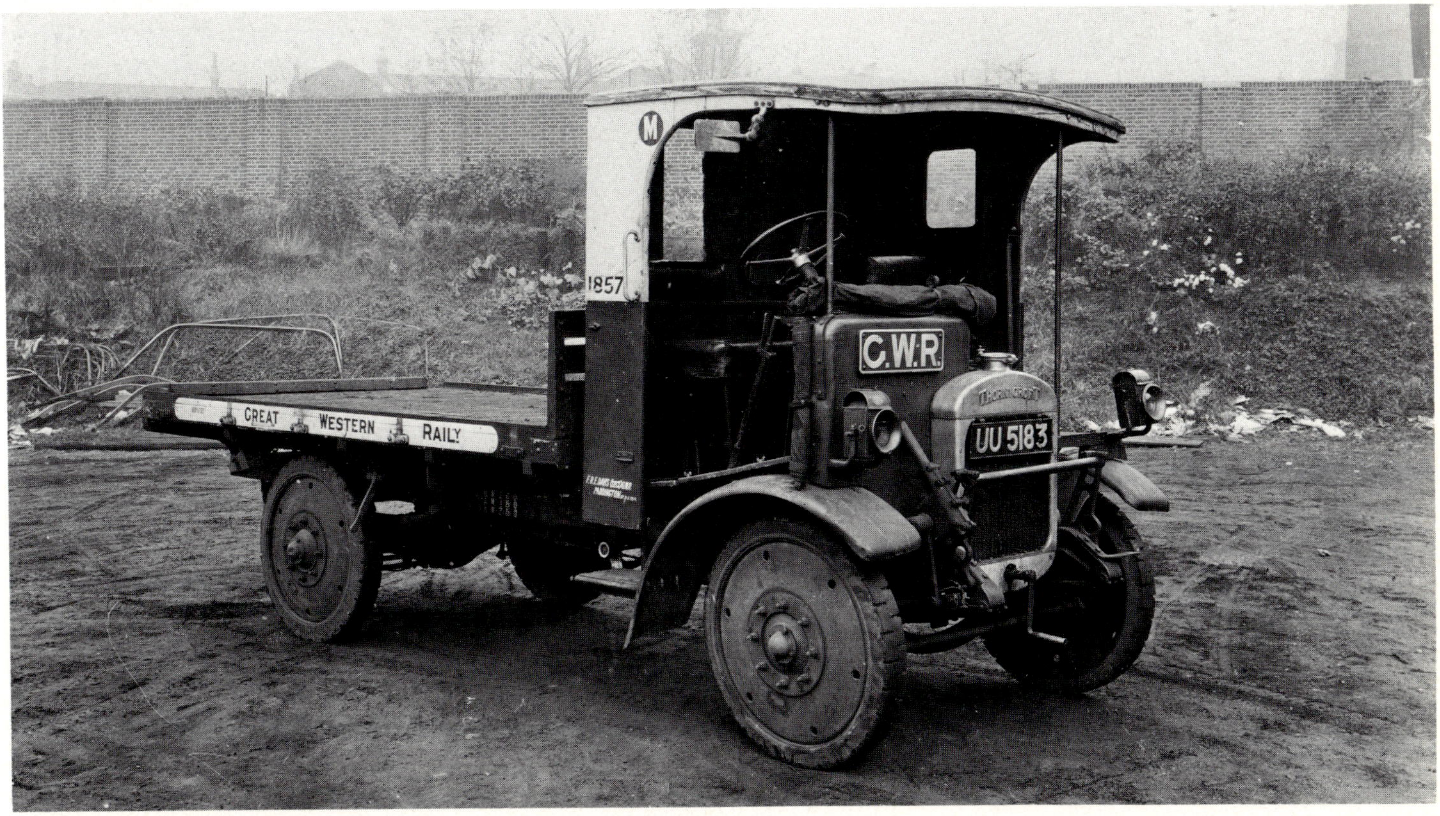
M
1857
G.W.R
UU 5183
GREAT WESTERN RAILY

G.W.R
THORNYCROFT

G.W.R
1007
G W R
EXPRESS
CARTAGE
SERVICES

Plate 61:— The Great Western Railway took delivery in 1929 of a hundred 30 cwt forward control A.1. chassis from John I. Thornycroft & Co. Ltd. The top photograph shows the vehicle at their Basingstoke works, under test on 1 November 1929, in temporary works livery and stencilled "G.W.R." on cab front.

Plate 62:— No. 2007, one of the above chassis, after Swindon Works had completed the van body and painted it ready for the road. In this instance the cab had been built by the chassis manufacturers. It seems, at this time, that the lighter vehicles were fitted with pneumatic tyres. Photograph taken at Swindon works on 4 December 1929.

G.W.R.— Thornycroft Forward Control A1 Parcels Van

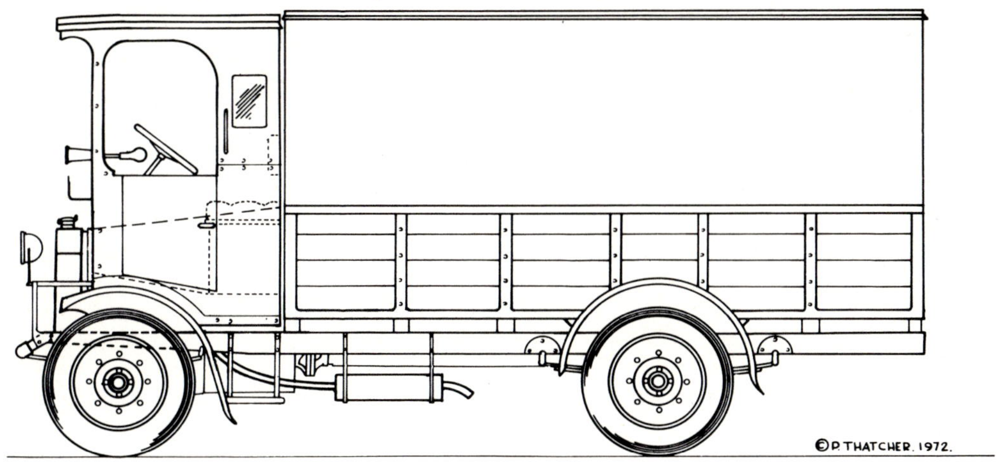

Scale 7mm/1ft

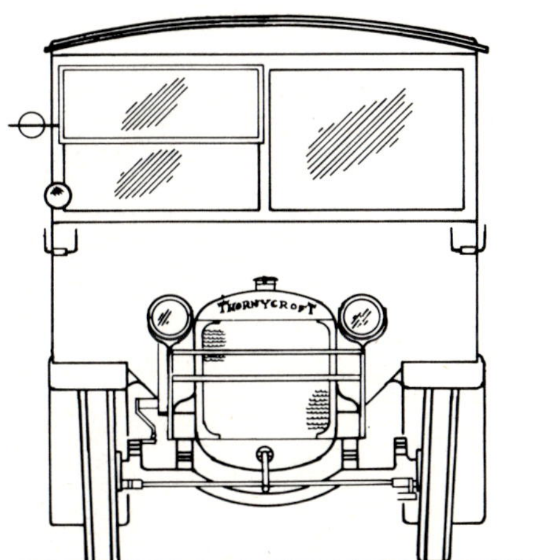

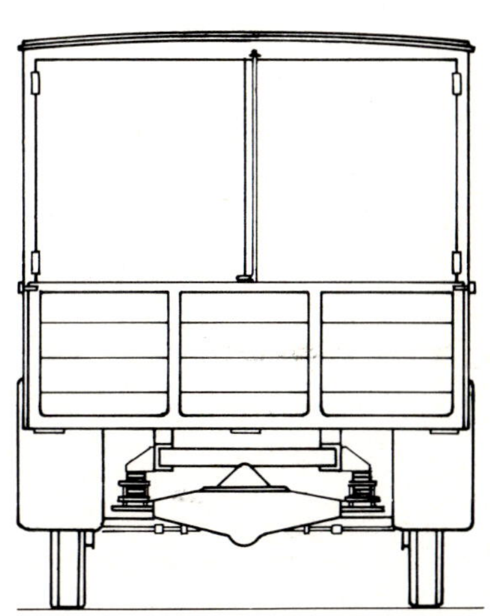

FEET

Plate 63:— In 1929 it became apparent that equipment capable of hauling heavier loads, in some districts of the G.W.R., was required. Shown here is S.18, a 12 ton six-wheeler steam wagon built by Fodens Ltd., Elworth Works, Sandbach, Cheshire, loaded with grain at Exeter in typical British weather on 6 December 1929. During 1929 four rigid frame six-wheelers were supplied to the G.W.R. Two were fitted with flat platform bodies 20ft long, as above, and two with hydraulic 3-way tipping bodies. They were designed for loads of 10-12 tons at 12mph or for gradients of 1 in 7 at corresponding speeds. The boiler worked at 220lb per sq.in. The total heating surface was 90sq. ft. and the compound engine had 4¼" and 7" diameter cylinders with 7" stroke but it could be worked with live steam in both cylinders and independent exhaust when required.

Plate 64:— As well as the 30 cwt. chassis ordered from Thornycroft's a hundred 4 ton forward control chassis were delivered to the G.W.R. in 1929, thereby making it one of the largest orders of this kind placed with the manufacturers. This picture shows one of the 4 ton chassis under test at Basingstoke on the 1 November 1929, prior to delivery to the G.W.R. Solid tyres appear to be the order of the day for this weight of vehicle at this time.

Plate 65:— One of the above chassis fitted with a G.W.R. flat body, with removable sides. This vehicle number 1716 bears a Swindon paint date of 26 November 1929 and was photographed in October 1930. Brackets were fitted onto the sides for the tarpaulin hoops as shown.

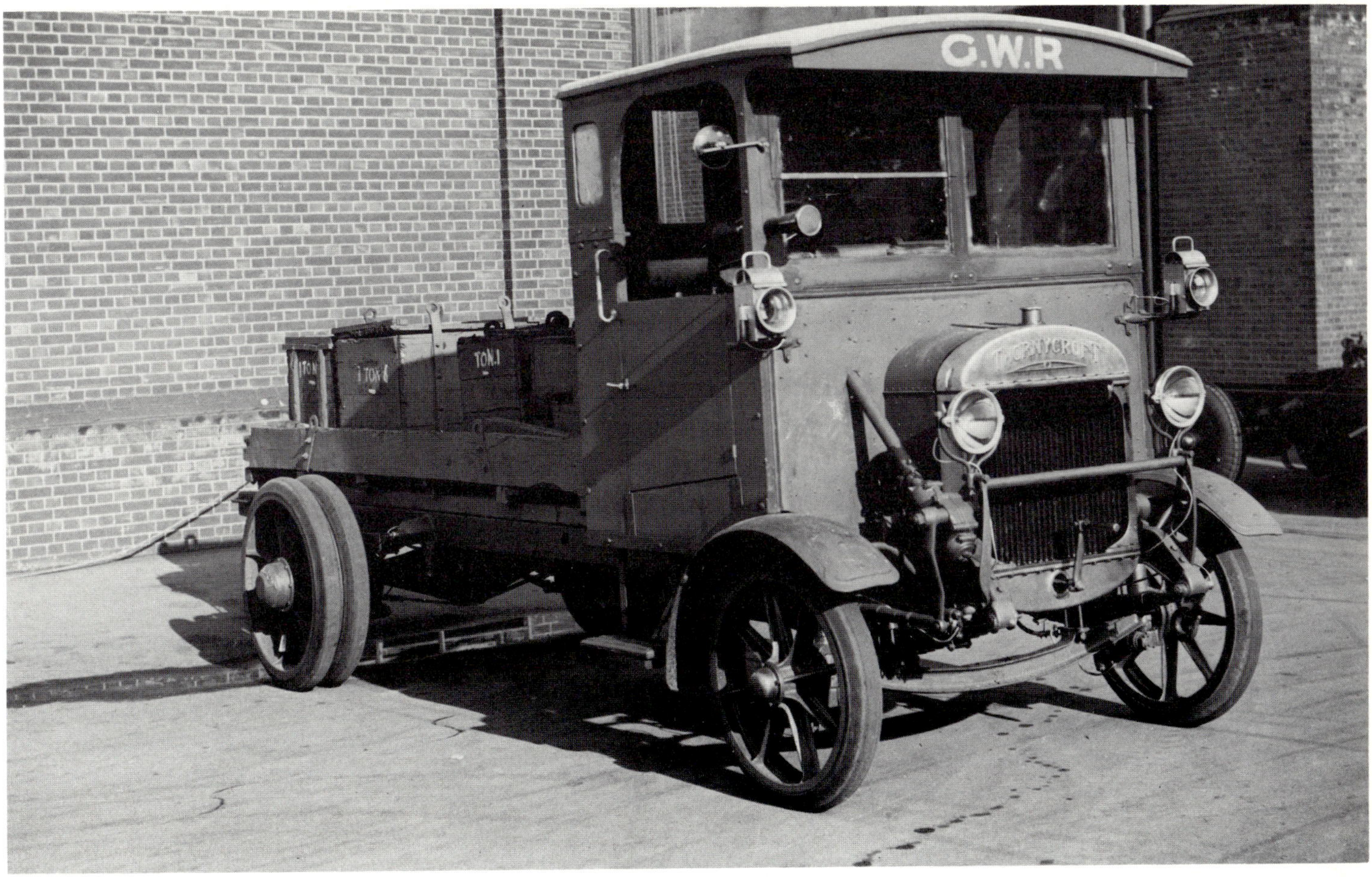
G.W.R

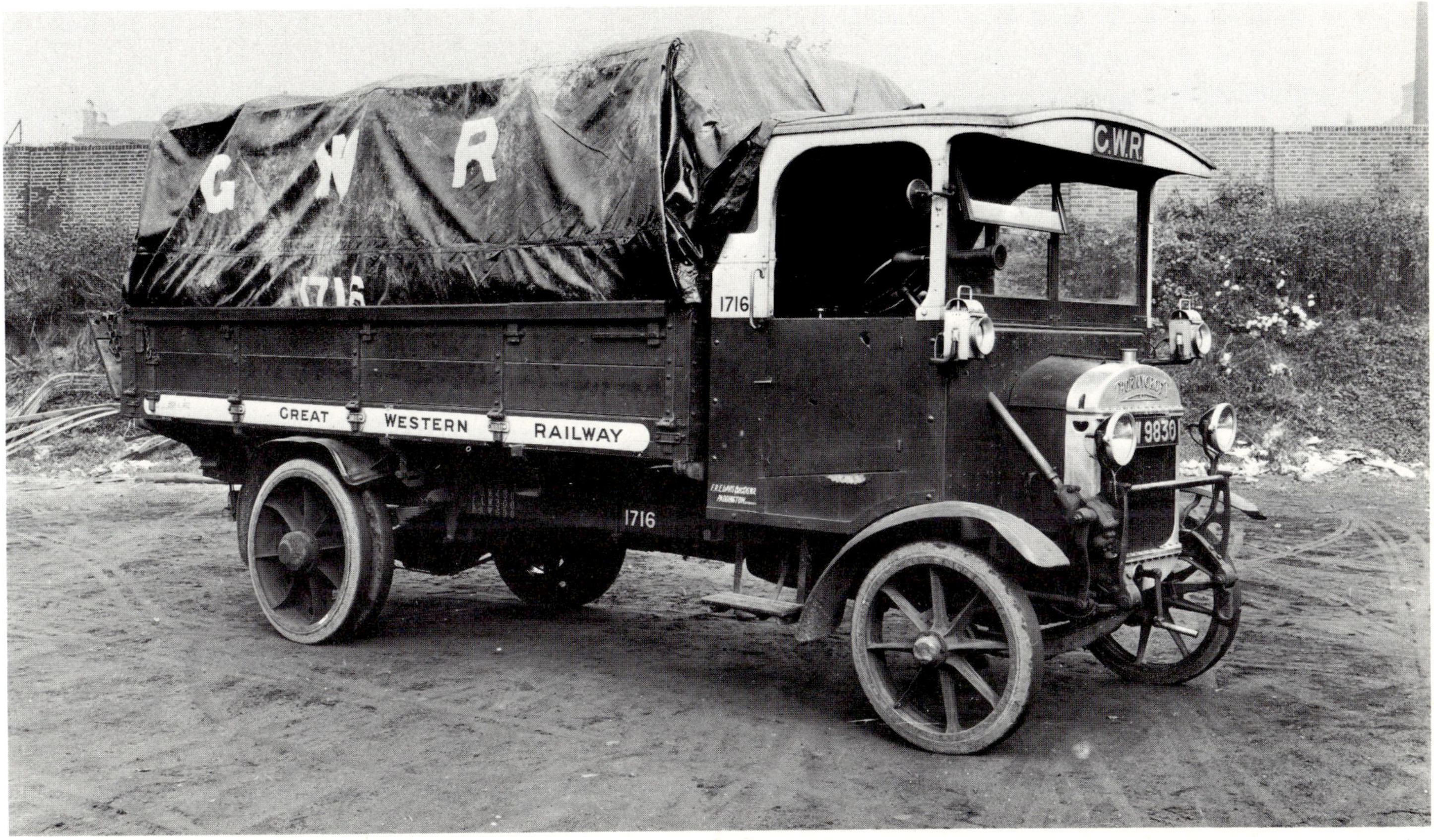
G W R
1716
G.W.R
1716
GREAT WESTERN RAILWAY
1716
9830

Plate 66 and *Plate 67:—* Contract hire par excellence. No 979 a 30 cwt Thornycroft chassis with Swindon body painted in MacFarlane, Lang & Co's own livery, thought to be green. Photographed at Bristol on 12 December 1928. Fitted with footsteps and handrail to enable the driver to reach the roof rack — quite a job with a handful of 7lb empty biscuit tins! As can be seen in the lower picture one way to see out of cab during wet weather was to open the top section, there were no windscreen wipers fitted. Petrol filler cap shown next to windscreen; petrol tank was above dashboard.

Plate 68:— G.W.R. fleet number 1938, a 4/5 ton Associated Daimler chassis fitted with Swindon flat body and removable sides. The paint date was 8 March 1929 and photograph taken at A.E.C. works at Southall shortly after. It is interesting to note that the Daimler Motor Co. Ltd joined forces with A.E.C. from 1926-1929 making Associated Daimler vehicles. After the later date Daimler concentrated on passenger vehicles. In this photograph it is noticeable that the offside door is held shut by a piece of wire attached to the mouth of the horn! No electric lights or windscreen. Fitted with solid rubber tyres. The tarpaulin hoops are shown grouped together in front bracket for use if required.

Plate 69:— Vehicle No. 1910, a 4/5 ton Associated Daimler chassis with Swindon flat body, paint date 1 May 1929. Shown here adapted for milk traffic and standing in the Station Yard at Shrivenham on 2 October 1929. This lorry was fitted with pneumatic tyres and full windscreen. As this vehicle probably did a lot of work in the dark (carrying milk), it is shown fitted with acetylene lamps. The petrol tank was under the driver's seat, hence the pipe in cab side with hefty cap secured by wing nuts.

G.W.R.
875
GREAT WESTERN RAILY
SPEED 20 M.P.H.
K 3805

286
GREAT WESTERN RAILWAY
G.W.R.
G. W. R.
YH 979

Plate 72:— Due to the increase in the Company's cartage and the greater diversity in the loads carried, different types of road vehicles were required. At the end of 1929 there were 287 motor units in service. The vehicles shown here are a pair of 10 ton tractors, numbered 1082 and 1080, built by Scammell Lorries Ltd. of Watford, with permanently coupled trailers fitted with high sides, at the premises of the St. Martin Preserving Co. Ltd., Slough Trading Estate on 23 September 1929. Did the sacks carry manufactured pips for the raspberry jam?

Plate 70:— This peculiar looking Burford 30 cwt. forward control flat lorry No. 875, with detachable sides, photographed at Swindon Works on 22 February 1930, was the result of a rebuild from an omnibus type similar to one shown on page 112. Using the same chassis the bus coachwork was removed and a cartage body fitted in its place. Many of the G.W.R. motor omnibuses were converted in this way. This particular vehicle was finally withdrawn and scrapped in 1933. The word railway is again shown abbreviated. Petrol tank under seat.

Plate 71:— Another rebuild, this time an A.E.C. 3½ ton chassis with flat body No. 286 converted in 1927. The picture on page 108 shows how this vehicle looked as a charabanc. Fleet numbers were retained after conversion. This photograph shows the lorry in the goods yard at Torre on 27 May 1930 loading agricultural machinery for the Bath and West and Southern Counties Show at Torquay.

Plate 73:— A six-wheeled forward control P.B. Thornycroft chassis fitted with full cab and hinged high sided body. The unladen weight is shown as 7ton 3cwt 2qrs. This vehicle was photographed on 14 April 1930 and, judging by the roof board, was also used for St. Martins Preserving Co.'s traffic. Close scrutiny of the picture shows that the vehicle was fitted with one windscreen wiper on the driver's side only. The livery looks like all over brown. Photograph taken on front hill Paddington.

Plate 74:— As previously mentioned, the Great Western Railway was engaged in the cartage of gravel and sand from the jointly owned pits at Theale in Berkshire. One contract required the conveyance of 5000 tons. A large number of high sided vehicles were required for this traffic and the majority were purchased from Messrs Thornycroft. The photograph on this page shows a superb collection of road vehicles of this type assembled at Theale Station in 1930. Front Row — left to right — Foden steam wagon; tractor and trailer, Thornycroft 10 ton six-wheeler. Remainder mostly 4 ton Thornycrofts with solid rubber tyres and 1 Associated Daimler on extreme right.

Plate 75:— Theale and Great Western Sand & Ballast Company was the name given to the joint concern working the pits and conveying the material. Here is shown vehicle No. 2247, a 7 ton Thornycroft chassis fitted with a 6½ cu.yard capacity steel hydraulic tipping body. The unladen weight shown on the cab is 6 ton 4cwt. Photograph taken on 6 October 1931 depicts the vehicle tipping ballast on site during construction of Tilehurst reservoir, Reading.

Plate 76:— No. 1077, a Thornycroft J.C. 10 ton six-wheeled forward control chassis fitted with side tipping steel hopper body at Theale Station on 6 October 1931. Note protective slats over petrol tanks. Considering the date this was a very modern looking vehicle.

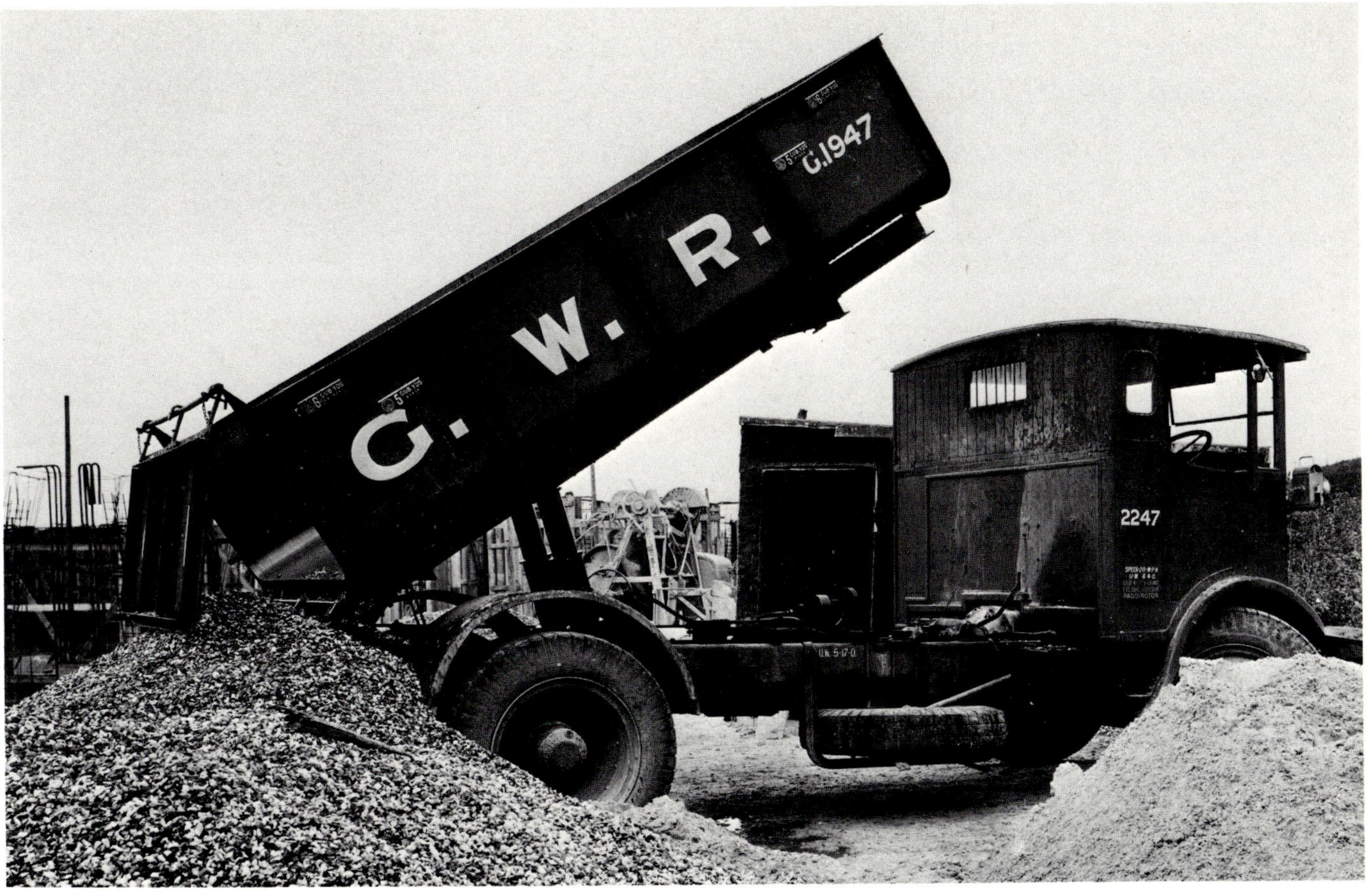
G. W. R.
G.1947
2247

GREAT WESTERN
G.1058. RAILWAY
1077
GC 3683

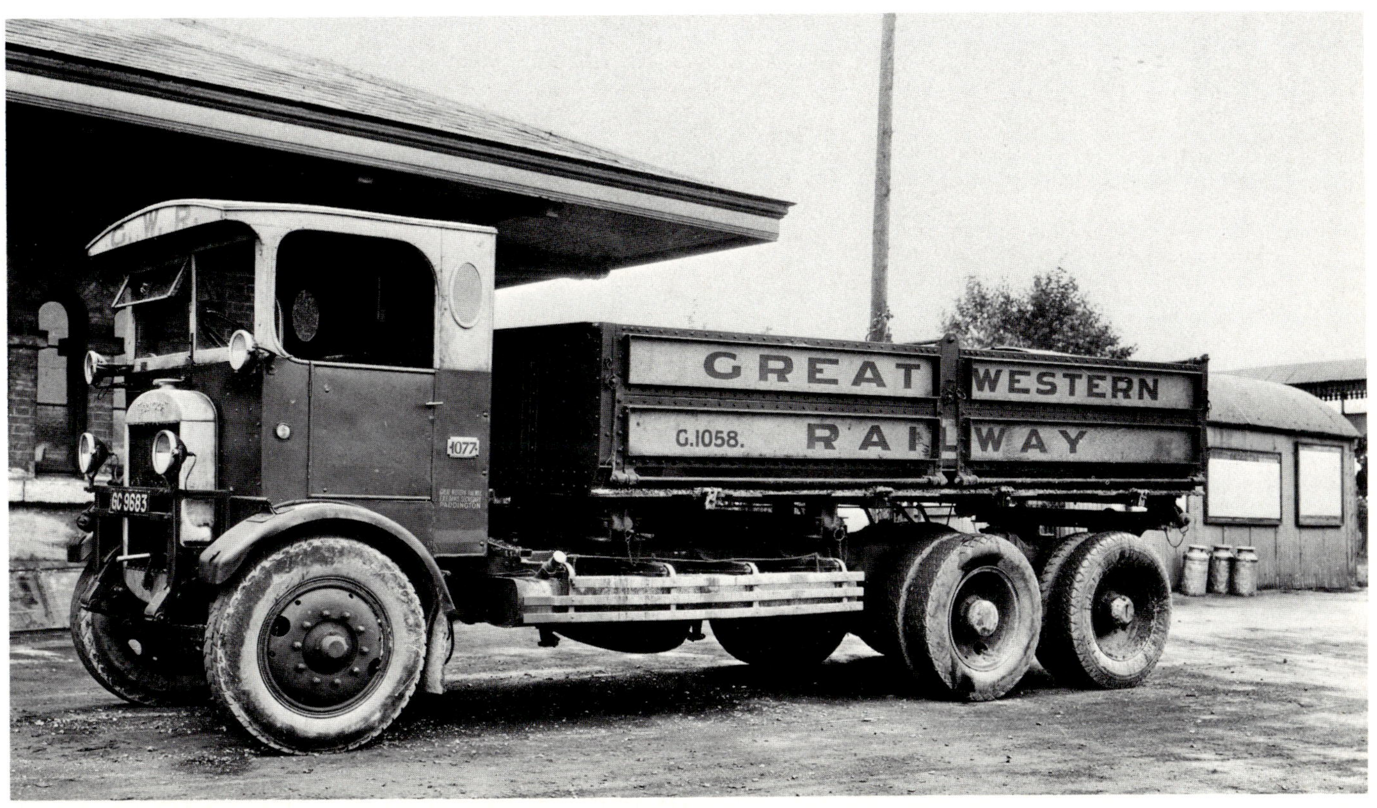

Plate 77 and *Plate 78*:— Two views of consecutive numbered Thornycroft J.C. forward control six-wheelers Nos. 1078 and 1079. These had a 32 cwt. body, with sides that were detachable, built at Swindon. The chassis was of 6 ton 1½ cwt and the engine was 6 cylinder developing 45.9 hp. When ordered in 1930 the cost recorded as £1400 each. The top photograph was taken at Swindon on 30 August 1933. Lower photograph taken at Swindon about 1935.

Plate 79:— During 1931 the G.W.R. still further extended their road freight services and took delivery of 219 new motors and tractors ordered at a cost of £127,000. Of these 108 were built by Dennis Bros. Ltd., Onslow Works, Guildford. They were 20.36 h.p. with forward control. This photograph shows the Dennis chassis being tested on a gradient of 1 in 6 on one of the hills overlooking Guildford on 31 May 1931.

Plate 80:— At Lostwithiel, Cornwall, the Nestle Company set up a milk concentration depot during 1932. This building was erected in the G.W.R. Station yard, a site which was convenient for the receipt of milk by road from the farms and for rail despatch in bulk, in 3000 gallon glass lined tank wagons. The Nestle Company contracted with about 600 farmers for daily supplies of milk up to a total of 7000 gallons. The collection of this milk, each day including Sundays, from such a scattered area presented a big problem. This was solved by the G.W.R. taking over the whole contract from the 1 October 1932. There were nine other small centres co-ordinated with the scheme each having its own allocation of lorries. Lostwithiel, being the largest, had six vehicles. The road equipment used on the contract was almost entirely made up of 2 ton lorries. The photograph shows — left to right — Thornycroft 2 ton, Morris Commercial 'Courier' high sided 6 ton, two Thornycroft 2 ton, and on extreme right the special 6 ton Morris Commercial double-decked lorry for conveying 135 eight gallon churns used in the remote areas. The two ton vehicles carried about 50 eight gallon churns. Forty years later this sort of operation is carried out by the Milk Marketing Board entirely by their own road transport. British Rail carries only a very small percentage.

Plate 81:— A 2 ton forward control chassis, with specially adapted radiator fitted to combat overheating in hilly districts, built by Guy Motors Ltd., Wolverhampton provided with a Swindon van body and numbered 2350 in the G.W.R. fleet. Fitted with electric head lamps, electrified oil lamps and horn. Photographed in July 1931.

Plate 82:— Another interesting conversion this 2 ton Guy OND chassis shown here as a motor lorry with detachable sides provided by Swindon. Previously this vehicle was a saloon motor coach used by the Company between Paddington and Victoria (see page 120 for illustration). Fleet No. 1651 retained throughout. Photograph taken on 23 August 1933 after conversion.

Plate 83:— In pre-Second World War days the conveyance of cattle was the prerogative of Britain's railways but not today. The Great Western Railway were very alert to this traffic and in 1930 this special vehicle was constructed. Originally fitted with an omnibus body, this 30h.p. forward control Maudsley ML 3 4/5 ton chassis is shown here after conversion in December 1930. The vehicle had two decks for use in conveying small animals, and when required for cattle the top flooring could be removed.

Plate 84:— During 1935 the G.W.R. in conjunction with the L.M. & S.R. purchased the livestock haulage business of Smith Bros. at Knowle. C. 2538 was one of the 2 ton short wheel base Morris Commercial tractors fitted with 'Tasker' cattle van trailer taken over from Smith Bros., shown here at Swindon Works after renovation in July 1935. Of interest is the one piece windscreen, wiper and electric horn. The tractor had normal livery but the trailer was varnished wood with black ironwork.

Plate 85:— A 4 ton Morris Commercial 'Leader' chassis fitted with 3 cu yard capacity body. No. 4003 was photographed in November 1936. The interesting thing about this lorry was the fact that it had a moveable floor. The idea was to obtain a more efficient substitute for the tipping vehicle. The floor consisted of a rubber band extending over the whole length and width of the lorry wound over a roller at each end. By the simple operation of winding from one end to the other, a load of sand or similar material could be discharged by hand very quickly. This picture shows the vehicle in what looks like works grey livery and it was probably used departmentally.

Plate 86:— This Fordson 2 ton chassis fitted with flat body and detachable sides was photographed in Swindon Works on 5 September 1934. No. 3174 shows a couple of points worth noting about livery. Cast plates of the words 'Great Western Railway' were placed on a cream strip. The GWR monogram was used from about August 1934 onwards and is shown here on one of the first road vehicles to bear it.

Plate 87:— Vehicle No. 2826 a Morris Commercial forward control chassis, with Swindon van body, photographed at that works on 15 September 1933.

Plate 88:— No. 2839, an almost identical vehicle to that above, except that this one has two licence holders in the cab, a requirement necessary under the Road and Rail Traffic Act 1933, as described in the introduction to this section. This photograph taken at Swindon Works on 30 November 1934.

Plate 89:— Way back in the early 1930's the G.W.R. ordered, for evaluation, two chassis fitted with diesel engines. This photograph, taken at Swindon on 1 February 1934, shows No. 2285 a Thornycroft 'Taurus' 6½ ton van with a body built by Swindon. This vehicle had an 28h.p. 4 cylinder compression ignition engine. The Brockhouse trailer carried a 4½ ton pay load, again a Swindon built body. Bearing in mind some of the massive vehicles on our roads today, this pair must have looked gigantic in 1934. Note the forward arrangement of bumper bar which enabled the body to come within legal requirements.

Plate 90:— No. 3406, a very modern looking vehicle by any standards, is this 6 ton A.E.C. 'Monarch' chassis with flat body, fitted with detachable sides built at Swindon. An innovation was the sliding door on the cab. The door handle is very reminiscent of the early G.W. passenger rolling stock. A Swindon works photograph taken on 26 October 1934.

Plate 91:— Vehicle No. A. 3839, a 2 ton Morris Commercial forward control chassis with Swindon built flat body with detachable sides. Photograph taken at Swindon on 17 February 1938. Vehicles were supplied by the G.W.R. to the G.W. and G.C. Joint Committee and bore brown and cream livery.

Plate 92:— A. 2770, a 3 ton Thornycroft 'Nippy' chassis with flat body fitted with detachable sides. The cab and body built at Swindon with sliding door on offside only. Photographed at Swindon works on 2 June 1939.

Plate 93:— A 30 cwt Scammell lorry No. S. 4600 propelled by a 10h.p. twin cylinder air cooled engine situated beneath the body, which gave ample clearance for all maintenance purposes. A joint effort by both Scammell and the Great Western is shown here at Slough road motor workshops on 28 January 1938. The fitting of the engine in this position enabled the cab to be of easy access for the driver. This work was made much easier when delivering many consignments, such as small parcels, to many addresses. Note collapsible starting handle.

Plate 94 and *Plate 95*:— 25/30 cwt. Morris commercial van No. A. 4007. Body built by G.W.R. at Swindon, paint date 6 December 1938; photograph taken on 8 December 1938. Although a joint cartage vehicle, livery was brown and cream. In order that neither Company had preference, the front view shows L.M.S. first, rear view shows G.W. first! The grey panel was provided for current Q.R. posters to be billposted.

L.M.S.&C.W.
EXPRESS
CARTAGE
SERVICES
L.M.S.&C.W.
A4007
4007
EYL 825

C.W.&L.M.S.RAILWAYS
C.W.&L.M.S.
EXPRESS
CARTAGE
SERVICES
A4007
4007
EYL 825

Plate 96 and *Plate 97:—* 3 ton Thornycroft 'Nippy' van No. A. 3205, body built at Swindon to Lot 834 and photographed on 21 November 1945. Sliding door fitted to offside only. These vehicles proved to be a very efficient addition to the fleet and gave good service.

Plate 99:— In 1940 the Great Western Railway was asked by the H.M. Office of Works to remove Malvern College's 140 tons of effects from its temporary quarters at Blenheim Palace back to Malvern. Delivery was required to 25 different addresses. In all 76 vehicles were collected together from adjacent stations to carry out the exercise. Many different types were used including containers. An idea of this can be obtained from the photograph taken at Blenheim Palace on 1 August 1940. On extreme left a 2 ton Thornycroft No. A 2553, with utility body and trailer, normally used for farm traffic; next A.2640 a 2 ton Thornycroft 'Handy' flat with removable sides; in the rear a 4 ton Thornycroft cattle van.

Plate 98:— Two 4 ton Thornycroft vehicles in a very picturesque setting, both fitted with flat bodies carrying 4 ton capacity containers. It is interesting to note that the right hand lorry, with registration No. GC 9156, also appears on page 50 fitted with sides for gravel haulage. This photograph was taken at Wexcombe Manor near Marlborough, on 30 September 1937 during a household removal — another facet of the Great Western Cartage Department.

GWR

GF 9029

Plate 102:— During April 1920 the G.W.R. started the construction of a motor vehicle garage and workshop at Alfred Road, Westbourne Park, in West London. It consisted of 3 bays, overhauling, machine shops and stores. A separate building contained offices, kitchens and messrooms. The floor space of the bays was 188 feet by 143ft 6in. The photograph of the interior was taken on 10 July 1934. This garage was demolished a short time ago and the site is now covered by a concrete viaduct carrying the 'Westway' link to the A.40.

Plate 100 and *Plate 101*:— The Great Western Railway purchased All Saints Church in Tyndall Street, Cardiff in 1901. It was used in turn as a power house, an oil store and a biscuit warehouse. In 1929 the Road Transport Department took it over for use as a repair shop and garage. What was the vestry became the Foreman's office and stores. The altar area became an inspection pit, and instead of seating 400 people the building accommodated 12 motor lorries and associated workshop equipment. One hopes that all repairs were carried out very religiously and not left to providence! Photographs taken on 14 May 1936. Note the tyre which was moved during the exposure.

Plate 103:— As mentioned previously, the arrival of the mechanical horse and trailer brought a revolution in the cartage business. Up to 1935 the practice of replacing horses by motor vehicles was followed as the occasion appeared justified but from then on a policy of completely motorising certain stations was started. Two types of articulated vehicles were available, 3 ton and 6 ton with a tractor of 10h.p. and 14h.p. respectively. These were admirable for the purpose in mind. With the comparatively small expense of the bodies it was possible for one motor unit to be employed on an unlimited variety of traffic and could be attached or detached at a moment's notice. Photograph shows a 6 ton Scammel 3 wheel tractor with a Dyak G trailer complete with 4 ton capacity container on a typical removal job at Hanwell on 20 November 1936.

Reproduced from Great Western Railway Magazine

Plate 104:— As previously stated, experiments were started in 1931 with 3 wheel motor tractors towing horse drawn vehicles on short distances only. This photograph taken in 1931 shows a Karrier 'Cob' tractor, fitted with 9h.p. petrol engine, coupled to what looks like a flat body complete with rear wheels from a motor lorry, the differential having been removed.

Plate 105:— No. 2735, a typical 3 ton mechanical horse and trailer built by Scammell Lorries of Watford. Photograph taken in middle 1930's near their factory. The tractor was powered by a 10h.p. engine. The trailer was fitted with detachable sides and ends.

Plate 106:— Another vehicle of the same type as above but in this instance built for the G.W. & G.C. Jt. Railway and had the L.N.E.R. dark blue livery. Fleet No. was J.19.

Plate 107:— A larger version of the 'Cob' than shown on page 67, this 3 ton type built by Karrier Motors Ltd, Huddersfield, was used alongside the Scammell. A cob is a short legged sturdy horse, an apt name for this type of tractor it was thought. No. C.4104 was photographed at Swindon works on 23 February 1937.

Plate 108:— 3 ton Scammell trailer fitted with Swindon built half tilt body, type Dyak U, No. T.1167. Paint date 27 October 1936. Photographed 29 October 1936.

Plate 109 and Plate 110:— 6 ton trailer No. T.1267 built by Messrs. Crane and fitted with Scammell coupling. Designated type Dyak G by G.W.R. shown here after painting in standard livery on 15 April 1937. Dyak was a telegraphic code name, similar to that used for rail wagons.

Plate 111 and Plate 112:— A 6 ton Scammell 3 wheel tractor No. C.6289 at Swindon works after emerging from paintshop. Paint date 26 January 1940. Photographed on 28 January 1940. White edged mudguards and bumper to comply with blackout regulations in World War II.

GWR
C6289
FYU 11

GWR
C6289
FYU 11
GWR
G.W.R. PADDINGTON STATION LONDON

Plate 113 and *Plate 114:* – 6 ton Scammell trailer with Swindon built half tilt body, type Dyak O.J. No. T.1783. Photographed at Swindon works on 21 June 1938.

G.W.R.— Scammell 6-ton Tractor with Dyak OJ Trailer

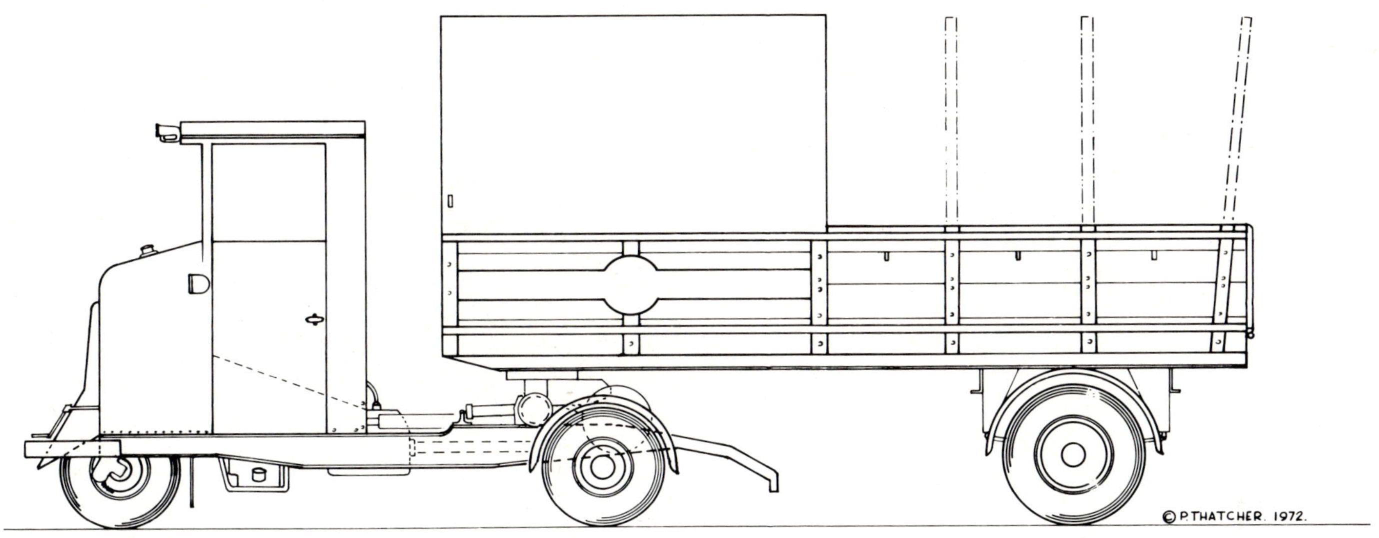

Scale 7mm/1ft

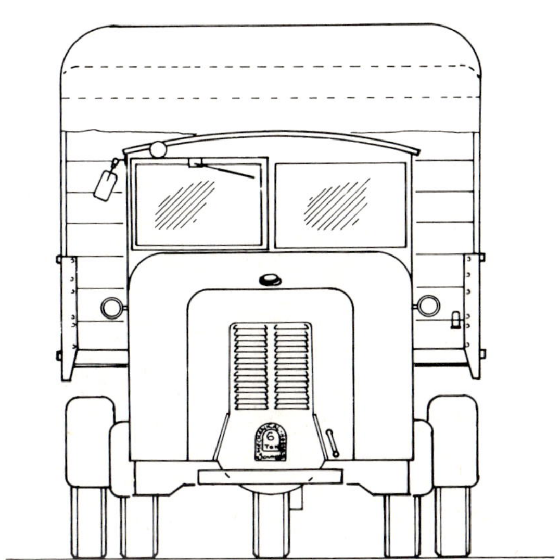

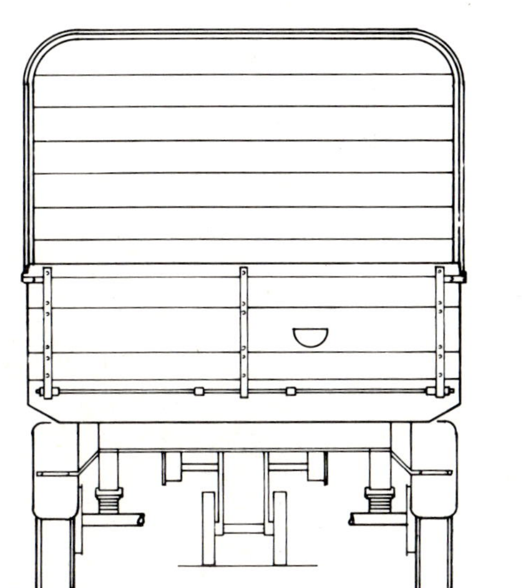

FEET

Plate 115 and Plate 116:— 3 ton Scammell trailer with Swindon body No.
T.1679, designated type Dyak O.H. Paint date 22 August 1938. Photograph
taken shortly after.

Plate 117:— Thornycroft 'Nippy' 4 wheeled tractor No. S.8816 with haulage capacity of 8 ton. Swindon built cab with sliding doors. Paint date 25 July 1940. Cab very similar to that on vehicle No. A2770 (see page 59). This tractor had the same coupling as the 3 wheeled type. White edged wings, the requirement for blackout regulations during World War II.

Plate   118:— A 3 ton Karrier 'Cob' and two 3/6 ton Scammell tractors with Dyak F trailers distributing Anderson shelter parts, from Westbourne Park yard in April 1939, prior to outbreak of second World War. Note three licence holders in cab, extra one for trailer.

Plate 119:— The year 1922 was the time when the G.W.R. carried out trials with an adapted Fordson tractor, supplied by Messrs. A & S Andrews Ltd, Ealing Common, London, which took the place of the more usual horse. The tractor was attached to an ordinary horse lorry and worked between Paddington and Victoria & Albert Docks, a distance of 14 miles. The idea was to devise a means to reduce the detention of an ordinary motor vehicle while being loaded or unloaded. Photograph taken on 22 June 1922.

Plate 120:— In 1918 the G.W.R. carried out experiments in the use of a combination motor lorry, which consisted of a powerful internal combustion engined tractor, working in conjunction with 2 wheeled semi-trailers. The 'Knox' tractor was imported from the U.S.A.; the adapted trailer partly built at Swindon and partly built at Slough was fitted with hinged legs.

Plate 121:— Owing to the increase in the traffic of cable drums, pipes and sugar beet, more tractors were required for hauling the special trailers. This picture shows a Fordson tractor with an Eagle trailer at Bampton on 26 October 1926. One supposes that as the rear wheels bear the initials M-H this item was supplied by Massey Harris.

Plate 122:— Fordson tractor with Eagle trailer, specially adapted to carry cable drums. Photographed in 1937.

Plate 123:— Fordson tractor with trailer adapted for conveyance of sugar beet in 1927. Tonnage of commodity carried in that year was 10,000 tons.

Plate 124:— A tractor built by McCormick-Deering Co., Rock Island, Illinois, U.S.A. hauling a trailer with a 20 ton load in 1927. When this photograph was taken this tractor was the only one of its type in Great Britian used for cartage work.

Plate 125:– An Eagle 4 ton trailer No.T.137, with solid rubber tyred wheels, specially designed for conveying containers and for haulage by tractor. Note interesting road and rail vehicles in background. Picture taken on 14 November 1934 at Hockley Basin, Birmingham.

Plate 126:– A 6 ton low loader trailer No.T.109 designed for tractor haulage at West Bromwich on 14 November 1934. Very nice 'Blake' P.O. wagon in background.

Plate 127:— A pneumatic tyred Fordson tractor and solid rubber tyred trailer No.T.81 awaiting the loading of a 4 ton BX container on 24 April 1929. This trailer was known as the 'Harrow' trailer and was built by the Harrow Industrial Co. Ltd., Green Lane Works, Stanley Road, South Harrow, Middx.

Plate 128:— A pneumatic tyred Dyson trailer No.T.172 loaded with a 4 ton FX insulated container on 4 November 1932.

Motor Omnibuses

It is now well known that because the Great Western Railway thought that £85,000 was a large sum to spend on the construction of a light railway between Helston and The Lizard, a decision was made to run a 'Road Motor' service between the two points. The service started on 17 August 1903 and made history as the first Great Western Railway bus service. The two vehicles used were purchased from Sir George Newnes, who in May 1903 had introduced a feeder service between Ilfracombe and Blackmoor on the Lynton & Barnstaple Railway. Owing to the Police objecting to speeds in excess of 8mph he was persuaded to sell them to the G.W.R. These two Milnes Daimlers were of the wagonette type but were rebuilt later with enclosed bodies. Three trips were run between Helston and The Lizard, in each direction with intermediate stops at Ruan Major, Penhale, Cury Cross Lanes and Lemarth. The single fare was 1s 6d (7½p).

An official report, dated 2 September 1903, stated *"That on the previous week 668 passengers and some 20 parcels were conveyed. Receipts were £45 (an average of 17/10d (89p) per trip). On fine days there were more passengers than could be conveyed. A 3rd car is required. Since inauguration of service absolute punctuality has been maintained"*

When one considers what the road surfaces were like, full of ruts, extremely muddy in Winter and very dusty in Summer, the vehicles stood up to it very well. Owing to the very bad condition of the roads, the service was suspended from October 1904 to April 1905 as the G.W.R. considered an omnibus too expensive a vehicle to be used as a steam roller! The Helston Rural District Council refused to roll the road and, as apparently there weren't any steam rollers in Cornwall to do the job, the Great Western sent one of theirs to the Cornwall County Council to get the road back to a reasonable state. A fire at Helston Garage, which destroyed two vehicles, also delayed the resumption of services.

Incidentally the Helston-Lizard service, together with others instigated up to late in 1904, were run contrary to legal requirements. While the Locomotives on Highways Act of 1896 had done away with the man carrying a red flag, the Act only applied to vehicles under 3 tons in weight. As manufacturers could not produce omnibuses to comply with this requirement, advantage was taken of the fact that no regulations were in existence stating what should be included in the weight of the vehicle, this obstacle was surmounted by removing items of equipment and painting the chassis 2 tons 19 cwts.

The regulations were modified in 1904 to allow the use of vehicles up to 5 tons in weight without a pilot. Also as regulations under the Motor Car Act of 1903 had not been formulated, the first three vehicles in the G.W.R. had no registration plates.

During the first few years the Great Western held a very prominent position as the pioneers of motor services. Other Railway Companies also purchased road motors but never pursued their services quite so vigorously as the Great Western.

The policy in the beginning was to run omnibuses strictly as feeders, it being considered not prudent to run between places connected by rail, however circuitous the railway route might be. This resulted in people refraining from travelling except in cases of real necessity. Later experience proved that a direct service created traffic. All early services were separate establishments which greatly increased operating costs.

At the end of 1904 The Great Western Railway employed more omnibuses than London therefore the Company attracted attention and brought enquiries from all over the world regarding working results. From a small start in 1903, with two Milnes Daimler passenger vehicles, the Company had 34 by the end of 1904, 95 in 1907 and in 1927 the total had risen to 300.

About 1905 so many operators required motor omnibuses that it became increasingly difficult to acquire them. The London omnibus services absorbed nearly all that could be produced. The ideal requirement for the G.W.R. was the Milnes Daimler type which was regarded as their standard. Only a few were readily available and the Company had to be satisfied with Wolseley, Durkopp and Clarkson steam cars, all of which gave trouble. In fact it was seriously considered in 1906 that the G.W.R. should design and build their own omnibuses.

The fleet remainded fairly steady without substantial increase until the start of the 1st World War in 1914. During that war some services were relinquished to other companies who were prepared to run them. In 1919 the G.W.R. came under Parliamentary obligation to withdraw their Wolverhampton and Bridgnorth service as the Wolverhampton Corporation desired to operate it. However that body was not ready to take it over until 1923. By this time the service was firmly established and it was a considerable loss to the Great Western when it passed out of their hands in that year.

Serious competition grew steadily after the 1st World War when many small companies and independent owners sprung into existence and who in turn were absorbed by large concerns — all this proved very harassing to the G.W.R.

In 1925 the Great Western's rights to develop their omnibus services were questioned by the London & Provincial Omnibus Owners Association in respect of services in the West of England and North Wales and as a result agreements were entered into with the Devon & Cornwall Motor Transport and Crosville Companies.

The Western National Omnibus Company was formed in January 1929, and this combined the road services of the G.W.R. and the National Omnibus and Transport Company in Devon and Cornwall. Later the railway linked interests with the British Electric Traction Co. Ltd. In other areas of the Great Western system other absorptions of road interests took place with such concerns as Western Welsh, Crosville, Thames Valley Traction, Midland Red, City of Oxford and Bristol Tramways. On the last day of 1933 the last omnibus in G.W.R. brown and cream livery was handed over to the associated Southern National Omnibus Company at Weymouth. Thus ended, after almost 30 years, the history of the independent Great Western Railway road passenger services.

Plate 129:— A cartoon, of the Lampeter-Aberayron "Road Motor" as depicted by a local artist, which appeared in the Great Western Railway Magazine in 1907.

Plate 130:— Milnes Daimler Wagonette No.1 leaving Helston for The Lizard on a preliminary run on 15 August 1903, prior to the service starting on the 17th. Trouble was experienced with the gearbox on this trip owing to the fact that a part was missing — it hadn't been put in by the manufacturers!

Plate 131:— Milnes Daimler Wagonettes No. 1 (Right) and No. 2 (Left) at The Lizard on the 15 August 1903.

Plate 132:— Milnes Daimler Wagonette No. 1 at The Lizard on 15 August 1903. The engine was a 4 cylinder Cannstatt-Daimler giving 16b.h.p. at 800 revs. per minute. Sims Bosch Magneto ignition, engine governed by throttle. The drive was through a cone clutch gear case and a universally jointed propeller shaft to the differential and cross shaft. The gearbox was arranged to give 4 speeds and reverse from 3 to 14mph. The road wheels were driven from the cross shaft by pinion and large gears being fixed to the wheels. This arrangement was very noisy and upset the Metropolitan Police when similar vehicles were tried in London. Three brakes were fitted, one working on record speed shaft and the other two on drums fitted to the driving pinions. There was also a screw type brake for emergencies and for holding the car when it had to be stopped on a hill. Solid rubber tyres were used on all wheels, those on rear driving wheels were 6 ins wide. Body was open wagonette type with light roof having 20 seats inside plus two on driver's seat. Petrol from the rear tank was forced by the engine exhaust gas to supply the single jet carburettor. Plain bearings were fitted throughout and there were wick fed lubricators. The solid rubber tyres cost about £200 per set and it was common for one or more to leave the wheel in the first few hundred miles. However petrol was cheap at 4d (2p) per gallon.

Plate 134:— From 17 August 1903 until 17 October 1903 two open cars were run. From 19 October one luggage motor omnibus seating 18 passengers and carrying luggage and parcels was substituted for the winter traffic. This photograph shows No.1 as converted to an enclosed vehicle. The livery in this case appears to be just varnished wood.

Plate 133:— Milnes Daimler Wagonette No.1 leaving Helston on 17 August 1903, the first day of the service to The Lizard. A tablet was erected on Helston Station in 1953 to commemorate this event.

Plate 135:— Milnes Daimler double deck omnibus No.16 shown here on the Torquay and Paignton service on 22 August 1904. This service started on 11 July 1904. The driver appears to be sitting well back to keep out of the waves. Most of the omnibus bodies at this time were built by Messrs. Dodson.

Plate 136:— Milnes Daimler 20h.p. 'Jersey Car' No.19 at Slough in 1904. These vehicles were used mostly on private outings. As can be seen, a ladder was required to reach most of the seats.

Plate 137:— Milnes Daimler 20h.p. double deck omnibus No.7 at Slough Station in 1904. This vehicle was presumably on the Slough-Windsor service judging by the advertisements. The Windsor service started on 18 July 1904 to supplement rail service. Notice the board with the driver's name, C.L. Hayward, on it just under the vehicle number. G.W.R. livery is much more apparent here.

Plate 138:— Milnes Daimler 20h.p. single deck omnibus No.12 with roof luggage compartment at Slough in April 1904.

G.W.R.
SLOUGH, ETON & WINDSOR.
GREAT WESTERN RAILWAY.
SLOUGH STATION, HIGH ST, ETON & WINDSOR.
17
G.W.R.

THE LIZARD & HELSTON
20
A 6181

Plate 141:— Milnes Daimler 16h.p. motor single deck luggage omnibus No.26 at Swindon Works in May 1904. This vehicle is shown carrying a destination board for Albaston, Callington & Saltash. This service was in substitution of a private horse bus, to which the Great Western Railway had paid a subsidy of £156, and was started on 1 June 1904. This was one of the vehicles which had a white bonnet.

Plate 142:— Interior of Milnes Daimler omnibus No.26. The similarity between this and the London Underground is quite marked, particularly the straps for standing passengers. Photograph taken in 1904 at Swindon.

Plate 139:— Milnes Daimler 20h.p. double deck omnibus No. 17 at Slough in April 1904. Vehicle is shown as being on the Slough, Eton and Windsor service. Brake shoes have no wooden blocks attached.

Plate 140:— Milnes Daimler 16h.p. motor wagonette No.20 with roof luggage rack photographed at Swindon Works in 1904 after emergence from paint shop in superb Great Western livery. The picture is so sharp that it is possible to read the manufacturer's name on the tyres — Peters Union Frankfurt A.M.

Plate 143:— A line-up of Milnes Daimler 'road motors' at Slough Station in 1904. Left to right:— luggage omnibus, jersey car, 3 single deck omnibuses, double deck omnibus.

Plate 144:— Slough Station 1904:— 20h.p. Milnes Daimler vehicles. Left to right:— Jersey car No.19, single deck No.20 on Windsor service, single deck No.13 on Beaconsfield service, single deck No.5 on Beaconsfield service, double deck on Windsor service.

Plate 145:— Slough Station 1905. Vehicles left to right:— 24h.p. Straker Squire double deck (one man operation), 30h.p. Milnes Daimler double deck omnibus, 30h.p. Milnes Daimler single deck omnibus, 30h.p. Milnes Daimler double deck omnibus, 20h.p. Milnes Daimler single deck omnibus, Clarkson 20h.p. steam car.

Great Western Railway

MOTOR OMNIBUSES

BETWEEN

SLOUGH STATION, STOKE POGES,

FARNHAM & BEACONSFIELD

SLOUGH AND BEACONSFIELD—WEEK DAYS.

		A.M.	P.M.	P.M.	P.M.			A.M.	P.M.	P.M.	P.M.
PADDINGTON	dep.	9 15	1 0	5 5	6 35	BEACONSFIELD	dep.	8 45	12 25	4 30	6 30
SLOUGH	arr.	9 51	1 24	5 29	6 59	(White Hart Hotel)					
SLOUGH	dep.	9 55	1 30	5 30	7 0	YEW TREE INN		...	...	...	Via "One Pin" and Stoke
SALT HILL		...	...	(Via Stoke see below).	...	FARNHAM COMMON					
FARNHAM ROYAL	about	10 20	1 55		7 25	(Post Office)	about	9 0	12 40	4 45	
FARNHAM COMMON						FARNHAM ROYAL	„	9 5	12 45	4 50	
(Post Office)	„	10 25	2 0		7 30	SALT HILL		...	...	...	
YEW TREE INN		...	..		...	SLOUGH STATION	„	9 30	1 10	5 15	7 10
BEACONSFIELD (White						SLOUGH	dep.	9 38	1 17	5 30	7 14
Hart Hotel)	arr.	10 40	2 15	6 15	7 45	PADDINGTON	arr.	10 3	1 45	6 0	7 50

SLOUGH AND "ONE PIN" FOR HEDGERLEY via STOKE—WEEK DAYS.
(Also BEACONSFIELD via STOKE.)

		A.M.	A.M.	P.M.	P.M.						P.M.
PADDINGTON	dep.	7 45	10 10	2 0	5 5	BEACONSFIELD	dep.	...	...	...	6 30
SLOUGH	arr.	8 25	10 38	2 29	5 29	YEW TREE INN	„	...	...	...	...
								A.M.	A.M.	P.M.	
SLOUGH STATION	dep.	8 35	10 40	2 30	5 30	"ONE PIN"	dep.	9 5	11 30	3 25	6 50
STOKE GREEN		...	...	...	...	for HEDGERLEY					
STOKE CHURCH		...	...	...	...	STOKE COMMON		...	...	...	...
(Cross Roads)						(Fox and Pheasant)					
STOKE POGES VILLAGE		...	...	...	...	STOKE POGES VILLAGE		...	...	...	...
(Sefton Arms)						(Sefton Arms)					
STOKE COMMON		...	...	...	...	STOKE CHURCH		...	...	...	...
(Fox and Pheasant)						(Cross Roads)					
"ONE PIN"	arr.	9 0	11 5	2 55	5 55	STOKE GREEN		...	...	...	...
for HEDGERLEY						SLOUGH STATION	about	9 30	11 55	3 50	7 15
YEW TREE INN		—	—	—	...	SLOUGH	dep.	9 38	12 4	3 57	7 35
BEACONSFIELD		—	—	—	6 15	PADDINGTON	arr.	10 3	12 42	4 25	8 10

The Omnibuses will call at the intermediate places shewn. Passengers may also join at any other point on payment of fare from previous stage.

FARES:

BETWEEN	AND					
	Slough Station.	Salt Hill.	Farnham Royal.	Farnham Common.	Yew Tree Inn.	Beaconsfield.
SLOUGH STATION	—	2d.	6d.	8d.	9d.	1/0
SALT HILL	2d.	—	4d.	6d.	8d.	1/0
FARNHAM ROYAL	6d.	4d.	—	2d.	4d.	8d.
FARNHAM COMMON	8d.	6d.	2d.	—	2d.	6d.
YEW TREE INN	9d.	8d.	4d.	2d.	—	4d.
BEACONSFIELD	1/0	1/0	8d.	6d.	4d.	—

BETWEEN	AND						
	Slough Station.	Stoke Green.	Stoke Poges Church.	Stoke Poges Village.	Stoke Common.	"One Pin."	Beaconsfield.
SLOUGH STATION	—	3d.	4d.	6d.	8d.	9d.	1/0
STOKE GREEN	3d.	—	2d.	4d.	6d.	8d.	1/0
STOKE POGES CHURCH (Cross Roads)	4d.	2d.	—	2d.	4d.	6d.	9d.
STOKE POGES VILLAGE (Sefton Arms)	6d.	4d.	2d.	—	2d.	4d.	8d.
STOKE COMMON (Fox and Pheasant)	8d.	6d.	4d.	2d.	—	2d.	6d.
"ONE PIN," for HEDGERLEY	9d.	8d.	6d.	4d.	2d.	—	4d.
BEACONSFIELD	1/0	1/0	9d.	8d.	6d.	4d.	—

TICKETS will be issued on the Omnibuses, and must be retained until completion of journey.

BOOKS OF 24 TICKETS at the undermentioned reduced scale of charges can be obtained at the Booking Office at Slough Station:—

Between Slough Station and Beaconsfield	21/-
„ Slough Station and Farnham Common (Post Office)	14/-
„ Slough Station and Stoke Poges Village	10/6

FULL FARES TO BE PAID FOR ALL SEATS OCCUPIED.

TIME TABLES.—The Directors give notice that the Company do not undertake that the Motor Omnibuses shall start or arrive at the time specified in the Bills ; nor will they be accountable for any loss, inconvenience, or injury, which may arise from delay or detention.

BICYCLES will be carried, when they can be conveyed by the Omnibuses without inconvenience to Passengers, at a charge of 6d. each.

THROUGH RAILWAY TICKETS WILL NOT BE ISSUED ON, NOR BY, THESE MOTOR OMNIBUSES.

PASSENGERS LUGGAGE.—Hand Luggage will be carried free.

Heavy or bulky luggage which can be conveyed by the Motor Omnibuses will be charged for at the rate of 2d. or 4d. per package, according to size or weight, between Slough and Farnham Common (Post Office) or Stoke Common, and 4d. or 6d. per package, according to size or weight, between Slough and Yew Tree Inn and "One Pin" or Beaconsfield.

PARCELS.—Parcels will be conveyed by the Motor Omnibuses between Slough Station, Stoke Poges, Farnham Royal, Farnham Common, and Beaconsfield at the following rates :—

Up to 7lbs. in weight	**2d.**	7lbs. to 28lbs. in weight	**3d.**
28 lbs. to 56 lbs. in weight	**4d.**	56 lbs. to 112 lbs. in weight	**6d.**

PARCELS AGENTS.—Mr. Thos. Dunkin, Farnham Royal ; Messrs. Spong and Purser, Farnham Common ; Mr T. F. Lane, Beaconsfield.

For any further information respecting the arrangements shewn in this handbill, application should be made to Mr. W. A. Hart, Divisional Superintendent, Paddington Station.

Paddington, March, 1904.

JAMES C. INGLIS, General Manager

Plate 146:— timetable of 1904 Beaconsfield Service.

Plate 148:— 20h.p. Clarkson steam omnibus shown here in one of the squares near Paddington, London, prior to going into service. This vehicle was used with two others on the Wolverhampton — Bridgnorth service which started on 7 November 1904. These steam omnibuses gave considerable boiler trouble and were replaced by Milnes Daimlers. Prior to the steam omnibuses being sold they saw further service in Somerset.

Plate 147:— Milnes Daimler 20h.p. single deck omnibus, believed to be No.5, near Beaconsfield probably on the first trip of this service, which started on 1 March 1904. The diabolical road surface can be seen. Vehicle fitted with four oil head lamps.

Plate 149:— Milnes Daimler 20h.p. composite single deck omnibus No.8 at Helston Station in 1904. Note acetylene lamp on roof at front. This vehicle was placed on the service on 31 March 1904 for goods, mail and passengers (10 inside, 2 beside driver). The goods compartment could be used by passengers by means of flap seats. Smoking was allowed in this compartment.

Plate 150:— The above vehicle on Bochym Hill, near Mullion, between The Lizard and Helston in 1904.

Plate 151:— Avebury Halt on the Calne — Marlborough route which started on the 10th October 1904. This 20h.p. Milnes Daimler double deck omnibus is shown outside the 'Red Lion' in 1907. Apart from a few minor alterations this particular site has changed very little.

Plate 152:— Milnes Daimler 20h.p. double deck omnibus No.31 at Avebury, Wilts, outside the well known hostelry. Date about 1909.

Plate 153:— 20h.p. Dennis single deck omnibus No.158 outside the same public house at Avebury, Wilts, about 1911.

Plate 156:— Maudsley 14 h.p. 14 seat, single deck omnibus No.52 photographed at Slough in 1905. This was one of three vehicles ordered and was used on the Slough-Langley-Colnbrook service, which started 8 May 1905.

Plate 154:— From 1 May 1904 the General Post Office entered into a contract with the Great Western "Road Motors" to carry their mails between Helston and The Lizard. This photograph taken about 1912 shows one of the 20h.p. Dennis single deck omnibuses stopped at a road junction in order to exchange the mails with the local postman and his donkey cart.

Plate 155:— The same vehicle as above but this time at Ruan Crossroads with passengers disembarking.

Plate 158:— Straker Squire 24h.p. chassis fitted with an experimental front entrance double deck body built by G. Scammell & Nephew Ltd., Fashion Street, Spitalfields, London, E.1. This vehicle was used in the Slough area. It did not prove successful and was later fitted with a more conventional staircase. Photograph taken on 27 September 1905.

Plate 157:— Durkopp 20h.p. observation car or covered charabanc No.74, chassis built by Durkoppwerke A.G., Reinickendorf, Bielefeld, Germany, and photographed at Swindon Works on 24 August 1905. The body was built at Swindon to the design of Mr. F.C.A. Coventry, motor car assistant to the Supt. of the Line. The vehicle accommodated 30 passengers, and it was closed at the back by glass panels which obviated any inconvenience from dust. A cast plate on the front screen stated that the chassis was supplied by the Motor Car Emporium Ltd., London, W. this was also stamped on the front wheel bosses. These Durkopp vehicles were ordered because of the shortage of Milnes Daimlers as stated previously. The Durkopps were constantly in trouble with broken crankshafts and, because of the difficulty of obtaining spares, they were cannibalised to keep the remainder working.

Plate 159:— Swindon Works — Road Motor Shop on 25 July 1907. Both horse-drawn and motor vehicle bodies are shown. It is noticeable that the number plates are missing, therefore one may assume rightly or wrongly that, like steam locomotives, the body and chassis need not have remained together all their life.

Plate 161 and *Plate 162:*— As with everything else, the Great Western were very conscious of the impact of advertising. They hit on the idea of sending 'road motors' to various parts of the country to publicise places of interest on their system. These two pictures show a 30h.p. Wolseley double deck omnibus No.63 prior to setting off on one of these tours about 1908. On a similar tour a 'road motor' left Slough for Scotland on 4 November 1907 and reached Carlisle on 7 November 1907. From there its route was via Dumfries, Ayr Paisley, Glasgow, Crieff, Inverness, Elgin, Banff, Aberdeen, Dundee, St. Andrews, Stirling and Edinburgh. After this 2,479 mile tour, it returned to Slough early in 1908.

Plate 160:— One of the earliest Double Royal posters produced by the Great Western Railway to advertise their road motor omnibus services. It is almost certain that it was issued in 1907 to publicise the Llandyssil — New Quay service which started on 1 May 1907. The vehicle depicted is artistically represented as a 30 h.p. Milnes Daimler.

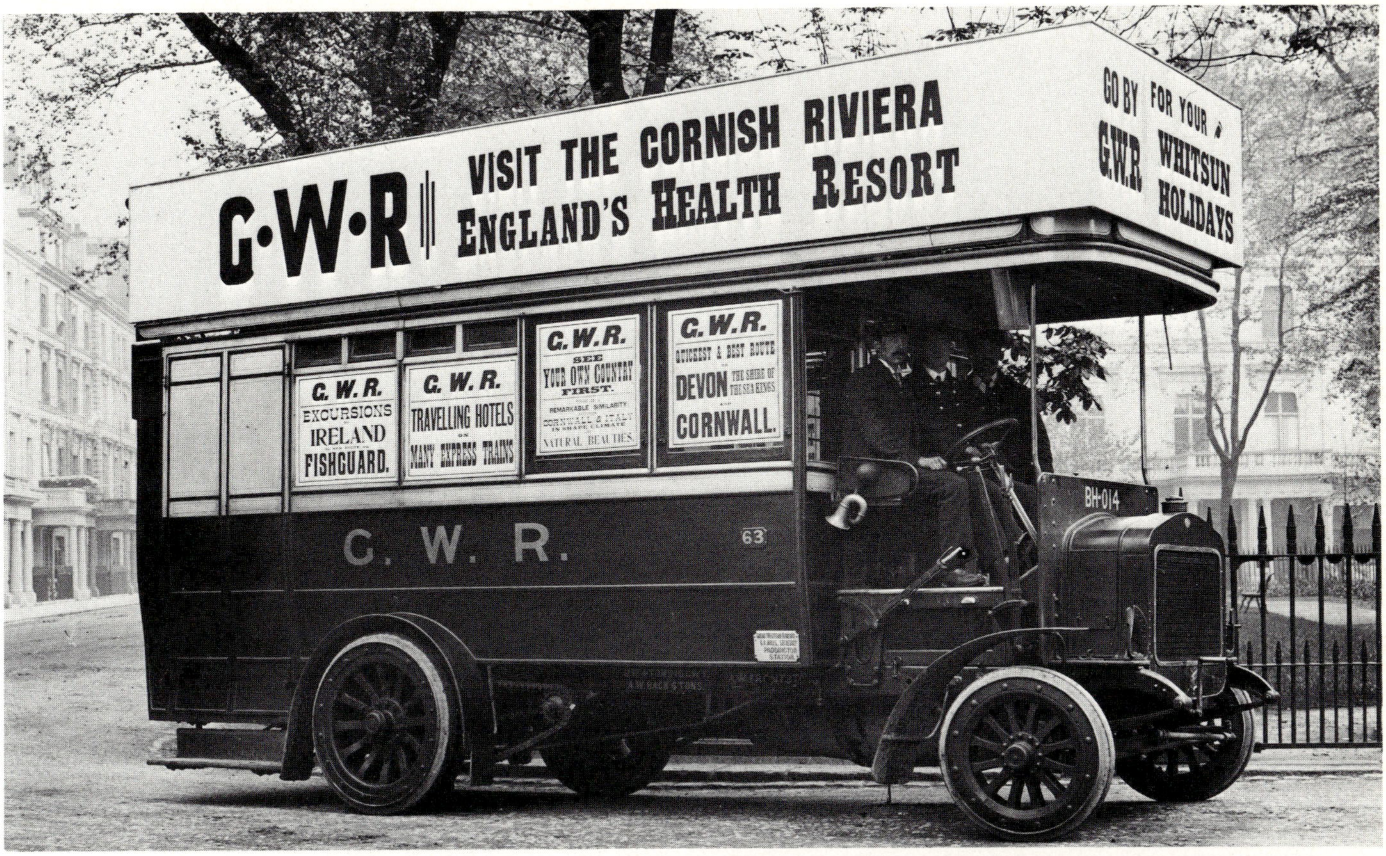
G·W·R
VISIT THE CORNISH RIVIERA
ENGLAND'S HEALTH RESORT
GO BY G.W.R.
FOR YOUR WHITSUN HOLIDAYS
G.W.R. EXCURSIONS IRELAND FISHGUARD.
G.W.R. TRAVELLING HOTELS ON MANY EXPRESS TRAINS
G.W.R. SEE YOUR OWN COUNTRY FIRST. REMARKABLE SIMILARITY CORNWALL & ITALY IN SHAPE CLIMATE NATURAL BEAUTIES.
G.W.R. QUICKEST & BEST ROUTE DEVON THE SHIRE OF THE SEA KINGS CORNWALL.
BH-014
G. W. R.
63

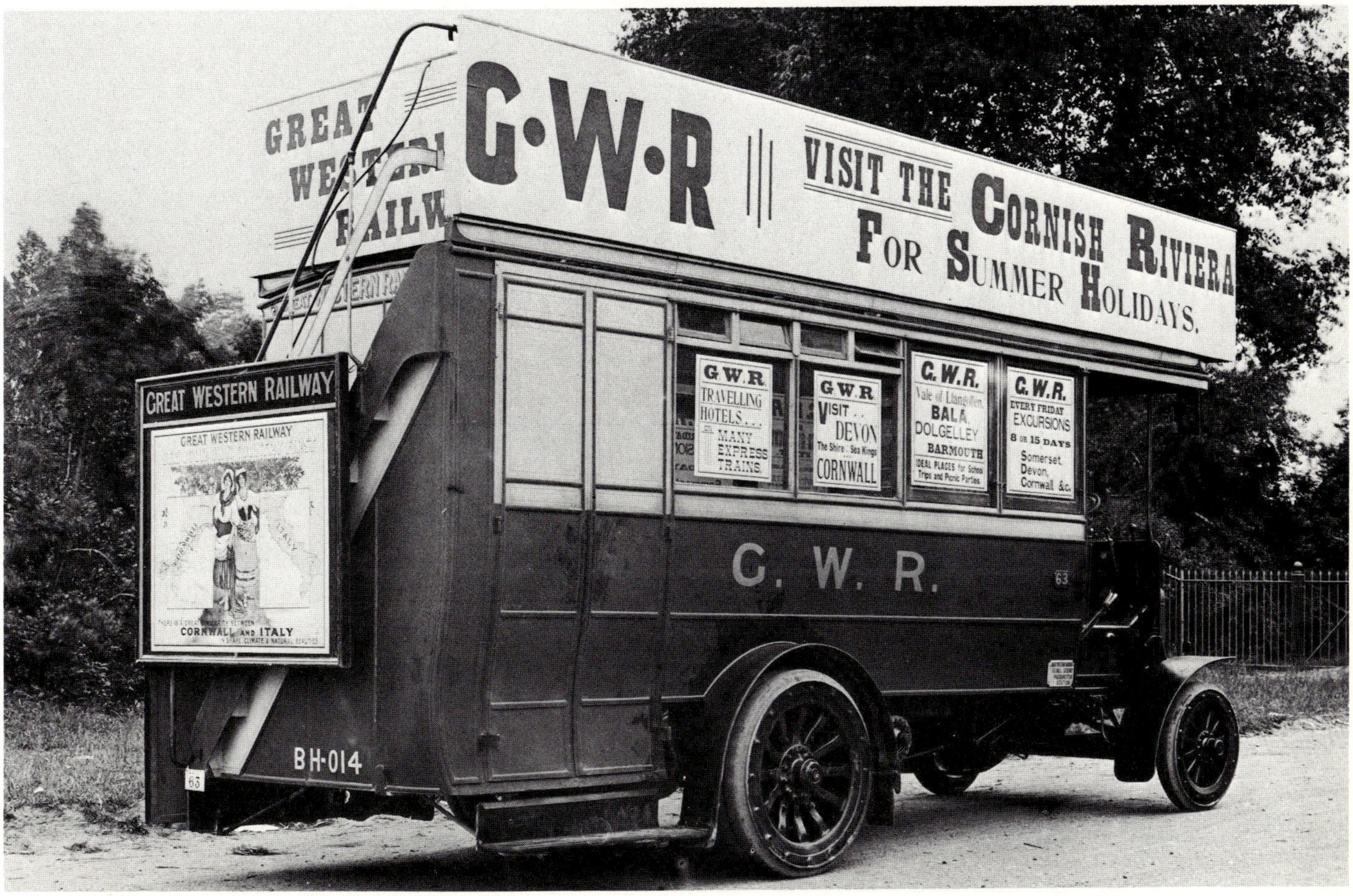
GREAT WESTERN RAILW
G·W·R
VISIT THE CORNISH RIVIERA
FOR SUMMER HOLIDAYS.
GREAT WESTERN RAILWAY
GREAT WESTERN RAILWAY
CORNWALL AND ITALY
G.W.R. TRAVELLING HOTELS... MANY EXPRESS TRAINS
G.W.R. VISIT... DEVON The Shire... Sea Kings CORNWALL
G.W.R. Vale of Llangollen BALA DOLGELLEY BARMOUTH IDEAL PLACES for School Trips and Picnic Parties.
G.W.R. EVERY FRIDAY EXCURSIONS 8 OR 15 DAYS Somerset, Devon, Cornwall &c.
G. W. R.
63
BH-014
65

Plate 163:— The G.W.R. had a great aptitude for using corrugated iron; one only had to look at their stations and halts to see the curious "pagoda" huts which grew out of the platforms. Another adaption is shown here. The G.W.R. Magazine stated in its issue of October 1908 *"The above photograph shows a new type of standard motor car shed which has been adapted. It comprises a car shed, stores hut, small workshop, office and is a considerable improvement on the former system of separate huts."* There was not much room in width or height and the top flaps were only opened for double deckers. This 20 h.p. Milnes Daimler is shown at Stroud.

Plate 164:— A glorious Summer's day at the Square, Llanstephan. The omnibus service between Carmarthen and here started on 1 May 1909. This photograph was probably taken just after that date. The driver appears to be standing under the lamp on the left hand corner. The vehicle is a 30h.p. single deck Milnes Daimler.

Plate 165:— Bell End Motor Halt on the Stourbridge — Bromsgrove route. This service started on 13 February 1905 between Stourbridge and Belbroughton and was extended to Bromsgrove in 1910. This picture gives an idea of what must have been a very typical scene on many of the Great Western Omnibus routes.

ALBION HOUSE, CARMARTHEN
GENERAL DRAPERY.
G W R
UNION HALL STABLES.
COFFEE TAVERN

Plate 166:— Milnes Dailmer 30 h.p. single deck omnibus No.41 fresh out of Swindon paint shop, (paint date 6 April 1910) ready to go on the road for another advertising tour. Photograph taken on 11 April 1910. One notices that the vehicle is fitted with shaft drive. The exterior brake acting on tyres of wheels has also been dispensed with.

Plate 167:— Dennis 20 h.p. single deck omnibus No. 156. Body built by Swindon Works. Paint date 23 May 1910. As can be seen the coachwork is very railway like in its appearance.

Plate 168:— Maudsley 35 h.p. charabanc No. 205 photographed on 28 June 1914. Fifteen of these Maudsley chassis were ordered in 1913 and were very successful; they were fitted with various types of bodies. A ladder, also numbered 205, was provided for easy access.

Caption overleaf

Plate 170:— This delightful rear view of the coal gas converted vehicle No. 213 as already described. Smoking was not allowed on top deck!! Not a very good forward view either! One wonders if the ZILVO advert was only displayed on gas bag vehicles.

Plate 169:— No.213 another 35 h.p. Maudsley chassis, this time with a double deck body and gas bag, at Slough. During World War I the G.W.R. adapted many vehicles to run on coal gas because of the shortage of petrol. The biggest difficulty, apparently, was keeping the gas bags anchored to the tops of the buses. In very windy weather some drivers had to chase their gas bags over fields. About 250 cubic feet of coal gas gave equivalent power to one gallon of petrol. It is understood that the firm of H.D. Bowyer is still extant.

Plate 171 and *Plate* 172:— A.E.C. 3½ ton chassis with enclosed single deck body, No 232, was photographed on 21 August 1923. As already described these ex-Army chassis were fitted with transferable coach or cartage bodies. This particular vehicle became a lorry in 1928.

232
C. W. R.
SPEED 12 M.P.H.
232

286
C. W. R.
286
SPEED 12 M.P.H

Plate 175:— Because the A.E.C. 3½ ton vehicles were rather large for some of the narrow roads traversed on some routes, there was a requirement for a lighter vehicle. An order was placed for 10 Chevrolets. This photograph shows one of these 22 h.p. 14 seat single deck omnibuses, supplied by Chevrolet Motor Co., Detroit, Michigan, U.S.A., at Slough on 30 August 1924. Note pneumatic tyres.

Plate 173:— Another view of No.232 taken at Swindon Works on 11 January 1923. The large saloon body was designed and built at Swindon. The ventilation was carefully considered, hinged droplights in front of and ventilators to the rear of the passenger compartment ensured a good current of air. The seats were made of light open metal supports instead of the wooden variety formerly used. Gangway hinged seats were installed which could be swung neatly under the main seats when not required. Electric lighting was fitted. There were trap doors in the floor to give easy access to parts of the chassis. Twenty-two vehicles with this type of body were built.

Plate 174:— A.E.C. 3½ ton chassis with charabanc body at Swindon in May 1924. Compare this picture with that on page 48 where the vehicle is shown as a lorry.

Plate 176 and *Plate 177*:— Two views of No. 806 a 23 h.p. Burford forward control chassis with Buckingham charabanc body. The front view with doors open looks a bit reminiscent of the broad gauge! Photograph taken at Kingsbridge in September 1924. This vehicle became a lorry in 1929.

Plate 178 and *Plate 179*:— No.813, a 23 h.p. Burford forward control chassis with Swindon built full front body on the Farnham Common service at Slough on 12 March 1925. H.G. Burford & Co. Ltd and the G.W.R. between them did much to develop the forward control system in order to give more body room on the chassis. This vehicle carried both electric and oil lamps. Note Hackney carriage plate on rear of vehicle.

Plate 180:– No. 859, another full-fronted body on a 23 h.p. Burford forward control chassis at Swindon on 10 May 1925. Compare with picture on page 48, not the same vehicle but one of the same type. This vehicle No. 859 became a lorry in 1928.

Plate 181:– In the Annual Report for 1926 from the Supt. of Road Transport which was presented to the Traffic Committee meeting on 28 April 1927, it stated that a shelter at Mathry cross was supplied by Messrs Pratten & Co. of Midsomer Norton at a cost of £22.10s.0d (£22.50) including erection. This was on the Fishguard-St.David's route. These shelters lasted for many years.

Plate 182:— No. 1202 a 30 h.p. Maudsley ML 3 chassis with John Buckingham 32 seat single deck saloon body, at Slough in 1927. This vehicle incorporated all the improvements at that time, such as pneumatic tyres, four wheel brakes and ground gears. This omnibus was sold to the Thames Valley Traction Company in 1931.

Plate 183:— No. 1280, a Guy FBB chassis with John Buckingham "all weather" type body, at Torquay in June 1927. These vehicles were increasingly used for land cruises such as to Dartmoor, North Wales etc. Eventually sold to Western National Omnibus Company in 1929.

Plate 184:— No. 1278, a Guy FBB chassis with a Vickers of Dartford, saloon body, at Torquay in May 1927. Sold to Western Transport, later Crosville in 1929.

Plate 185 and *Plate 186*:— No. 1229 Maudsley ML3B chassis with John Buckingham "all weather" body, at Bristol (Temple Meads) on 11 May 1928. Top picture shows hood closed, lower picture shows hood open. This vehicle is shown as designated for a land cruise but presumably not without its registration plates, which were YW 1721. Eventually sold to Thames Valley Traction Co. in 1931. It is interesting to note that the Station clock shows 12 noon in the top picture and 12.25 in the bottom picture. Did it take all that time to open the omnibus roof?

Plate 187 and *Plate 188*:— No. 1238 A Maudsley ML3 chassis with John Buckingham saloon body, fitted with above roof blind indicator box, at Slough on 14 May 1928. Note railway type roof ventilator and polished metal bonnet cover. Sold to Thames Valley Traction Co. in 1931.

Plate 189:– No. 1101 a delightful lightweight Morris commercial saloon omnibus at Swindon Works on 9 September 1928. Swindon built front entrance body, later rebuilt into commercial vehicle. Same chassis as vehicle on page 40.

Plate 191 and *Plate 192:–* Top picture shows exterior, lower picture interior, of No. 1298 Thornycroft A.6. chassis with "all weather" body at Swindon on 8 January 1930. This vehicle had a 6 cylinder engine and the maximum permittted speed was 20 mph. Fully fitted with both interior and exterior electric light. In the interior view one can see that the seating arrangement was very confined and the layout staggered.

Plate 190:– No. 1658, A Guy OND 2 ton 25 seater saloon omnibus with G.W.R. front entrance body at Swindon Works on 3 September 1929. Eventually sold to the Bristol Tramways & Carriage Company.

Plate 193 and *Plate 194*:— Two 30 cwt Thornycroft 25h.p. A.1. chassis fitted with Swindon built omnibus bodies at Swindon Station, prior to an advertising tour, on 7 April 1930. Both vehicles became lorries shortly after the tour was over.

G.W.R.— Thornycroft A1 Omnibus

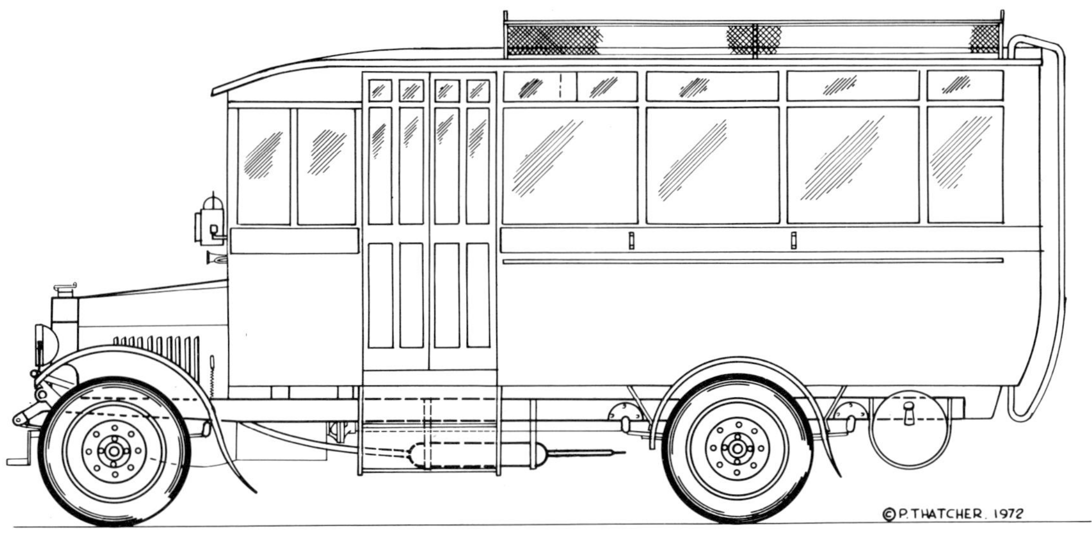

Scale 7mm/1ft

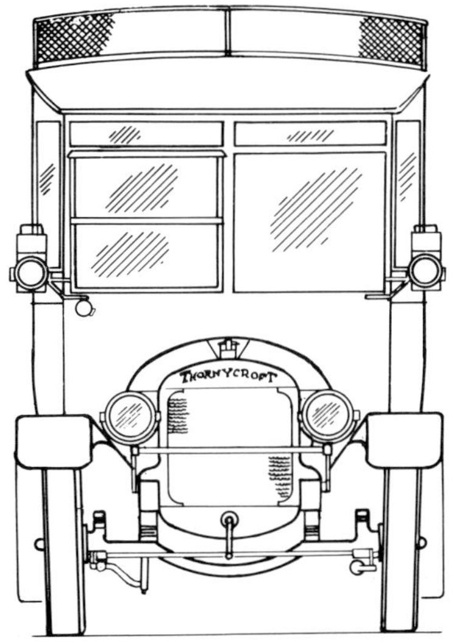

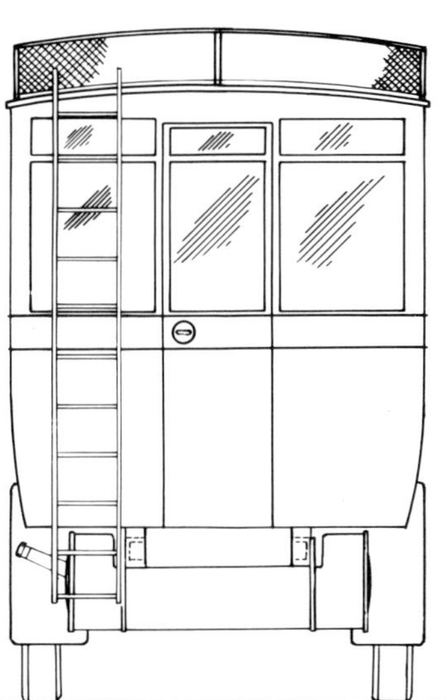

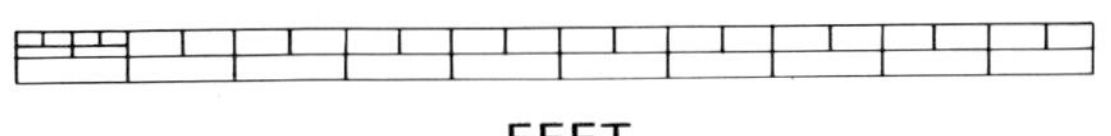

FEET

Plate 195:— A Guy OND 25 seater saloon No. 1651 on the Paddington — Victoria Interstation service in September 1930. This service was undertaken by two vehicles (numbers 1650 & 1651) carrying passengers booked through from the G.W.R. and the Continent and vice versa. London Transport took the service over later. Both 1650 & 1651 became lorries in 1933. On page 54 is a photograph of No. 1651 as a lorry.

Plate 196:— This picture is of a six-wheeled Morris commercial WD vehicle which was used for the Aberystwyth, Devils Bridge, Plynlimmon, Llanidloes service. The service from Devils Bridge via Plynimmon to Llanidloes started in July 1925. According to the G.W.R. Magazine, the 2 August 1928 saw the service start from Aberystwyth in the mornings. In the afternoons passengers travelled by Vale of Rheidol Railway to Devils Bridge where they joined the bus. The vehicle was a type used by the Army and had eight speed gearbox and was suited to running over rough country. The body was uncovered because a hood was not much use due to the very high winds. Every one of the 12 passengers carried were provided with an apron for protection against the mountain mists encountered on the high slopes. The vehicle was entirely controlled by the engine and brakes were only used for emergencies. This was the first excursion of its kind in England. Evidently the sign writer hadn't enough room to spell Plynlimmon correctly!

Miscellaneous Vehicles

Plate 197:— Illustrated is one of the three motor tricycle "auto carriers" which the Great Western introduced into London in 1910. One was used for express parcel delivery from Paddington, another for conveying advertising literature in the heart of London, and the third on parcel deliveries in the Acton area.

Plate 198:— In June 1926 the G.W.R., to meet the need for a cheaper unit for small collections and deliveries, introduced a number of "Carette" motor tricycle carriers on an experimental basis. These vehicles enabled the Company to give special services for urgent perishable consignments. The idea was to economise on transport by not using expensive equipment on all cartage. It is interesting to point out that the G.W.R. also used ordinary pedal tricycles on some duties.

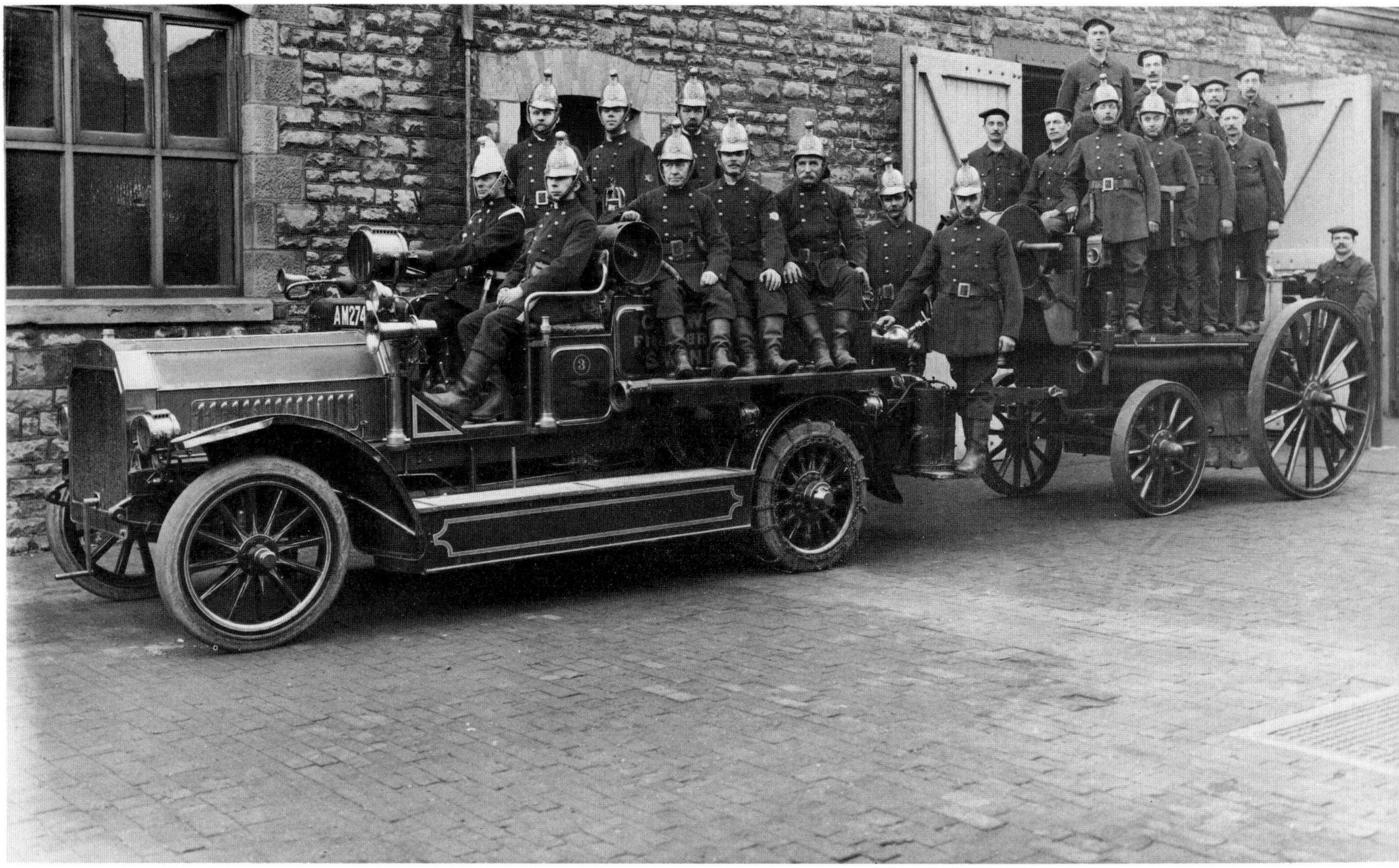
AM274

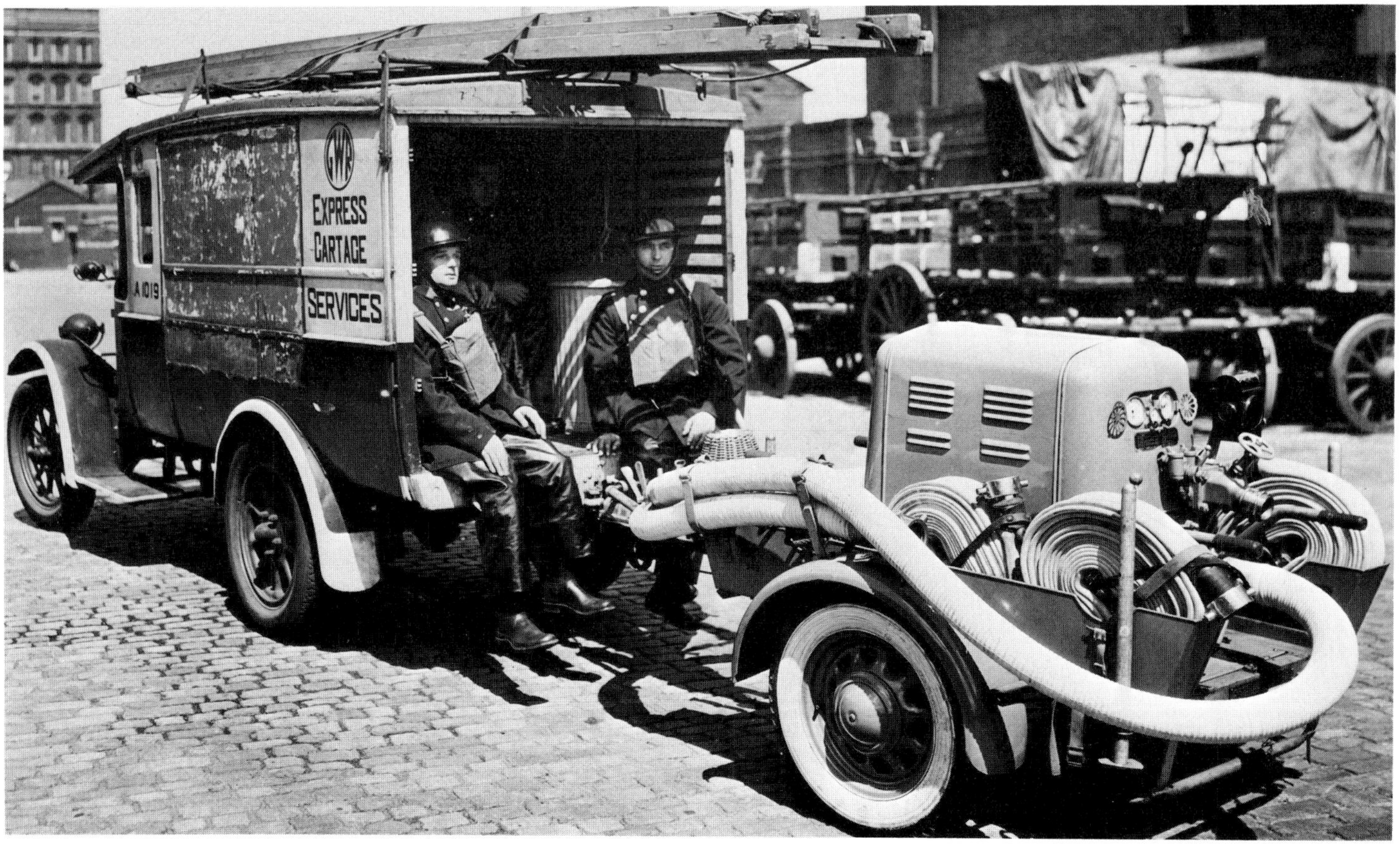
GWR
EXPRESS
CARTAGE
SERVICES
A 1019

Plate 201:— A 12 ton Foden six-wheeled rigid framed steam wagon No.S.17 at Swindon Works, shown here fitted with steam winch and condensing apparatus. The livery looks as though it could have been green with the appropriate lining. This vehicle was used on many diverse duties such as manoeuvring heavy loads, like boilers, onto low loaders.

Plate 199:— Fire precautions were always, and still are, a very high priority on railway premises. This photograph shows part of the Swindon Works Fire Brigade in 1916. The leading vehicle is a petrol engined fire engine built by Dennis Bros. of Guildford and being towed is a four-wheeled oil fired steam fire engine. Everything looks in very tip top condition, and they were even prepared for extremely bad weather judging by the chains on the back wheels.

Plate 200:— A very dilapidated Morris commercial van dragged off the scrap heap to convey fire fighting equipment and to haul a World War II fire trailer pump. On board, in July 1940, are trained firemen, members of the G.W.R. staff. The dustbin contained sand which was used on incendiary bombs.

Plate 202:— No. 2399, a 2 ton Morris commercial forward control chassis fitted with Swindon van body, in use as an emergency ambulance at Paddington in May 1940. Headlight is fitted with official mask as required by the 2nd World War blackout regulations and edges of wings etc. are painted white.

Plate 203:— No. 233 Daimler limousine converted into an ambulance at Swindon Works in 1941. It appears to be painted black and looks more like a hearse! Are the door handles off condemned passenger rolling stock?

Plate 204:— The Great Western Railway Company designed and constructed a mobile motor-trailer canteen which, when heavy air raids were experienced during World War II, could be sent to any town on the G.W.R. system where feeding arrangements were disorganised. Shown here at Paddington on 15 October 1941. It consisted of a 4-wheeled Thornycroft tractor hauling a 6 ton Scammell drop frame trailer with an overall length of 21 feet. The vehicle was designed at the Road Transport Department drawing office at Slough and constructed at the carriage and wagon shops at Swindon.

Plate 205:— A.285, a 20h.p. Austin limousine converted into an ambulance by the G.W.R. and shown here at Swindon Works on 15 January 1944. This vehicle was in the usual brown and cream livery. The registration number was very appropriate.

Plate 206 and *Plate 207:—* At the end of this album credit is given to the men without whom the Great Western Railway Road Services would not have got off the ground. The drivers particularly must have been a very hardy race, particularly in the very early days, without any protection at all from the weather. They also had to be mechanics as there were very few, if any garages along the routes to call on. These two photographs taken in April 1915 show the type of uniform in use at that time.

Left:— Motor driver complete with breeches and gaiters.

Right:— Conductor with ordinary suit similar to railwaymen.

Appendix I

Copy of Report to Traffic Committee dated 21 January 1904.

Motor car Services are now in operation between

		Distance
Road 1	Helston Station & Lizard	11 miles
Road 2	Penzance Station, Newlyn & Marazion	4½ miles
Road 3	Chalford & Stonehouse Stations	7 miles

Numbers of passenger carried to 31 December 1903

		Service commenced	Total Passrs.
1	Helston	17 August 1903	7,042
2	Penzance	31 October 1903	16,091
3	Chalford	12 October 1903	100,661

(*week ending 2 January 1904 working results:—*)

Service	Tfc. Receipts	Working Expenses	Car Miles Run	Receipts per mile	Working expenses per car mile
Helston	£413.13.6	£362.10.11	7,960	1s 0.48d	10.92
Penzance	£198.19.3	£205.17. 1	4,915	9.71d	10.05
Chalford	£819. 9.4	£363. 8. 7	14,011	1s 2.03d	6.22

Note:— for depreciation and interest £97.11.1 should be added to Helston expenses, £62.19.0 to Penzance expenses and £98.0.6. to Chalford expenses.

Appendix II

In the early days the drivers were paid in the following manner:

1 Standing money	—	21s to 29s a week
2 Mileage money	—	2d for every 10 miles run in service 4d for every 10 miles on Sunday.
3 Petrol Bonus	—	1d a gallon for every gallon saved over a consumption of 4 miles a gallon. 8 miles for light parcels vans.

DOMINE · DIRIGE · NOS
VIRTUTE · ET · INDUSTRIA

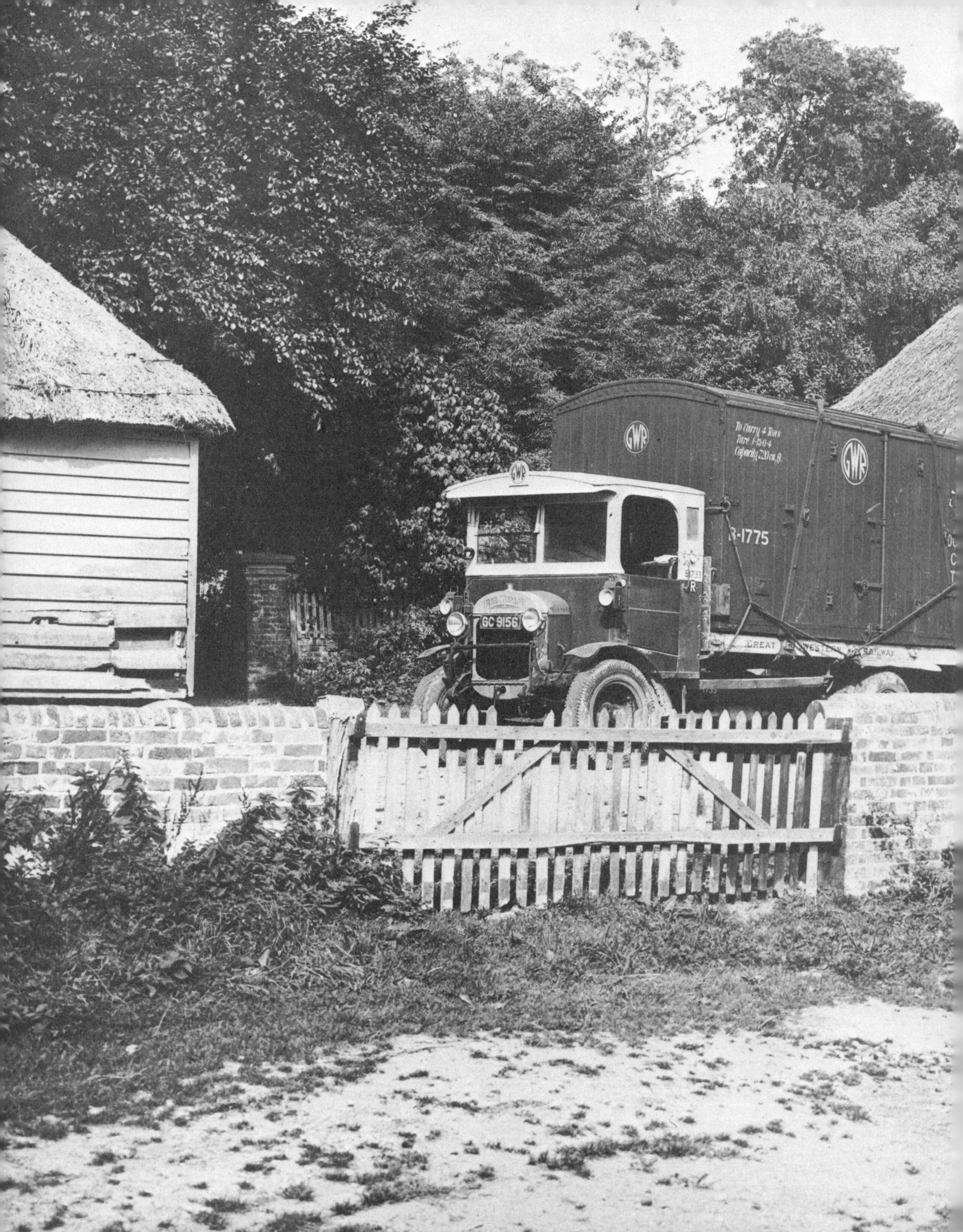

GWR
To Curry 4 Tons
Tare 1-8-0-4
Capacity 220 cu. ft.
GWR
R-1775
GC 9156
GREAT WESTERN RAILWAY